Discover Your Path

Your life is worth living

Luke Sheedy

DISCOVER YOUR PATH

Your life is worth living

LUKE SHEEDY

Copyright © 2013 Luke Sheedy

All rights reserved. No part of this publication may be reproduced, stored in a retrieval system, or transmitted in any form or by any means, electronic, mechanical, photocopying, recording or otherwise, without the prior written permission of the copyright owner.

The author of this book does not dispense medical advice or prescribe the use of any technique as a form of treatment for physical, emotional, or medical problems without the advice of a physician, either directly or indirectly. The intent of the author is only to offer information of a general nature to help you in your quest for emotional and spiritual well-being. In the event you use any of the information in this book for yourself, which is your constitutional right, the author and the publisher assume no responsibility for your actions.

Every effort has been made to determine and acknowledge copyrights, but in some cases copyright could not be traced. The publisher offers apology for any such omission and will rectify this in subsequent editions upon notification.

This book is a work of non-fiction.

Cover / Internals Design: Chhaya Joynt

Inner Knowing Publishing ™
www.innerknowingpublishing.com

ISBN 978-0-9874968-0-5

Dedication

This book is dedicated to Julia Sheedy, my beautiful wife who has helped me become the man I am today. We have lived many lives together and there's not a moment that goes by, I think how cherished and blessed I am to have her in my life. Julia, you're my Angel.

To Lorrie Lawler, you are a true sage who enlightens everyone who comes into contact with you. Thank you for coming into my life at the right time. You have been a major blessing.

The Ouroboros

The front cover features an illustration of the Ouroboros (pronounced or-bor-ous), a snake swallowing its own tail and forming a circle. It is one of the most ancient symbols in the world.

The Ouroboros has several meanings interwoven into it. Firstly, the biting of the tail is significant because it signifies the cyclical nature of life. It is also a symbol of transformation. You have the power to liberate and seek release from your thoughts, feelings and ideals which may have held you back all of these years, to become free and whole, so you can give birth to a new you.

The Ouroboros eats its own tail to sustain its life, in an eternal cycle of renewal. It's time to create what you want out of your life, and just like the cycles of life, we must be prepared for new experiences, change and growth, to be the best that we can be.

To me, the symbol is poignant as it signifies continuous renewal — the ability to recreate oneself, physically, mentally, emotionally and spiritually. We all have the ability to become a modern day alchemist, rediscover ourselves and create the life that we want, if we so choose.

By the time you have completed reading this book, you will never be the same again. Just like the Ouroboros, you will devour your old self and be reborn a new you.

Contents

	Introduction	1
1.	Where am I?	6
2.	Dreams	21
3.	Tomorrow land	30
4.	The past — stop going back there	41
5.	What are you up to?	56
6.	Enough with the excuses	64
7.	Change your thoughts, change your life	69
8.	Let the creativity flow	77
9.	Question time	88
10.	Are you listening?	104
11.	Your temple	112
12.	Money…it's just energy	124
13.	It's time for a spring clean…in your life	131
14.	What mask are you wearing today?	136
15.	It's time to reconnect…with people	141
16.	Happiness, it's not out there…it's in here	148
17.	It's time to self-actualise	155
18.	A spiritual tonic	158
19.	Death bed visions	161
20.	Your next chapter	166
21.	My best wishes	169
	It's time to believe in yourself	171
	Glossary	173
	Suggested reading	174
	Bibliography	175

Ask, and it shall be given to you;
Seek, and ye shall find;
Knock and it shall be opened to you.
For every one that asketh,
Receiveth,
And he that seeketh,
Findeth,
And to him that knocketh,
It shall be opened.
— *MATTHEW 7:7, 8*

To the reader

Well here it is! The book I promised you before we came here to this physical dimension.

The aim of this book is to help enlighten the path for you and help you discover all the hidden treasures within yourself. Are you ready to discover and share them with the rest of humanity?

The pact that you and I made was that I would encourage you to believe in yourself and you would find my book when you were ready to start living your life to its full potential.

I'm so glad you have kept your part of the bargain. Take only what you need from this book, stay true to yourself, love yourself and believe you are worthy of all the happiness and love in all of eternity.

Until we meet again.

Sincerely

Luke Edward Sheedy

Introduction

This life is worth living,
We can say, since it is what we make it.
— WILLIAM JAMES

It gives me great pleasure and joy to write this book for you because your life is worth living. It's to be used as a source of encouragement, for all people who are currently living on this planet. No matter which country you live in, or what part you are playing in it, to me we're all brothers and sisters, having an earthly experience. May this and the future generations, respond to this book with open arms. I have written this book from my heart to encourage you to believe in yourself, because you are most deserving. I believe in you.

I love life for all the ups and downs, the good times and the bad as these are the cycles that we go through, just like the seasons of nature, the tides of the ocean, the lows and the highs. You must learn to grow, change and adapt to your life changes, so you can turn negatives into positives and become a modern day alchemist. This is achieved by tempering your soul through your actions, thoughts and intentions and letting go of your self-defeating habits, routines and behaviours that keep your human potential limited. You will discover, like all true alchemists, you can transmute your life and manifest everything you want from life.

Simply by learning some new techniques and using the exercises included in this book, I know enlightenment and positive change can take place for you. This is a book of strategies for you to be happy now; however, you must play an active role in your life to get the most out of this book. Each chapter in this book will help you strengthen your character and soul to give you your worth to be happy and succeed.

It's time to discover you're a creator and it's you who shapes and forms your own reality by the thoughts, choices, decisions and actions you make every moment along your travels. Your life is in your hands. All your past jobs, challenges and experiences have laid the foundations for the person that you are today. With this book, you have the resources to turn your dreams into realities; it all starts with a belief in yourself.

My intentions for this book are to help enlighten the pathway for you, to guide, to push you, and give you encouragement to live your full potential and bring purpose and meaning back into your life. By opening up your mind and the new doors of reality, you'll find that it's you who has been holding yourself back all these years. It's time for you to rise above the ashes like the phoenix. You must be prepared for the big 'let go' and leap into the realms of higher consciousness. Don't be afraid. Feel the fear and continue. Let go of your defined boundaries and defined structures of thoughts and beliefs. Break your conditioning and programming that have held you captive like a caged animal. The truth shall now set you free; a new day is dawning for you. It's time to believe in yourself and your abilities, strengths and talents. Your dreams are no longer fictitious but reality and the incredible and unfathomable becomes possible.

The best thing about your life is if you want change, all you have to do is make the decision and act. You can start at any moment of your choosing, that's the beauty of it. When you come to the realisation that certain aspects of your life need to be improved and changed, and you're a willing participant, well you can begin right now, today. Every moment in your life is priceless and precious, and if you're still living, understand the possibilities and the opportunities of your life are infinite.

By exploring new dimensions of who you are and opening your mind to a new reality, you won't feel defeated by your thoughts and feelings anymore. Your new sense of self-awareness and freedom will tell you it's up to you how to respond to life's challenges. It's a choice you make. And when you make the decision to empower yourself you'll come to the realisation that your life is totally in your hands and you're in the driver's seat on the motorway of life. It's up to you if you want to make the most of it. Are you going to take the wheel or let someone else have control of your destiny and do the driving for you? That's a difficult question to answer!

This book will help you understand that it's you who controls your happiness, in whatever shape or form that comes in, materially, physically, emotionally, mentally, and spiritually. It will help you gain a new sense of happiness, freedom, and self-control. Your self-worth, esteem and confidence will be raised through the roof. It will give you the enthusiasm and direction to achieve anything and everything to which you put your mind to. The world is now your oyster. Don't you think it's time you became the director of your life, the master gardener of your soul's journey? Understand this, you're an infinite potential of creation, your life is yours for the making. It's time to become accountable, responsible and take the appropriate action in your life. Now believe in yourself, as I do.

It's my aim to share this knowledge and wisdom with you so you can benefit from what I have learned and you can reap the rewards and benefits of a happier, healthier and fulfilled life. We can all live the life of which dreams are made. When you do this not only will you benefit, but your family and friends and society will also receive the flow-on effects of what you have created through your positive mindset and actions. It will cause a ripple effect that benefits everybody in the community. You, my friend have so much more potential than you realise.

May I congratulate you on taking the next step in your life by choosing this book. As you know, the first step to change is always the hardest, but also the most rewarding as you have taken the initiative to start working on yourself and your life. I don't care about your age, race, colour or creed as long as you're willing and able, and you know within yourself you're ready to move onwards and upwards and you'll put your heart and soul into your new transformation. Nothing else matters because a new way of life awaits you. You're deserving and powerful beyond measure.

Stop your mind playing tricks on you, let go of the ego which keeps you separate from everyone and everything, it's an illusion. It's time for you to become part of the whole. You come from love, you'll go back to love, so it's time to do great things with your life and be love in service.

It's my wish that this book finds its way into everybody's hands, not just people who enjoy reading self-help, self-development and human potential books. Everybody can gain and enrich their lives for the better and contribute to the society in which they live. Remember this, you help no-one when you're not living to your full potential and living your life's purpose. However, you can help everyone and anyone when you've found your true calling and are happy and successful.

Read and re-read this book from cover to cover and take what you need from it. Underline parts of the book that you really enjoy and which strikes a chord with your soul. Answer the questions truthfully and honestly so you're participating as well. It will help identify areas in your life that needs attention and focus. You need to be an active, willing and enthusiastic participant. Be ready for your mind to be opened, to become more productive and discover your hidden talents, meaning and life purpose. It's time for you to achieve the happiness and success you so rightly deserve. There are no problems, only solutions. It's time your life changed for the better. Strengthen your inner vision and embark on your spiritual quest.

Live your life in a visionary way; let all of life's wonders be played out for you. Let the magic begin. Time is of the essence, it's in this moment when your life will truly unfold. Are you ready to truly express yourself in your own unique way, to discover your own hidden treasure? They will be found in the place you haven't looked yet — inside yourself. This is where your destiny awaits you, its time to tap into and reconnect with the source, your inner self. Listen very quietly with a still mind and your heart will tell you. Have the faith and courage to act now.

You are special, talented and gifted. Don't you think it's time you brought all the beautiful creation that you are to the surface and shine like the diamond that you are? Come and take this epic journey of self-discovery with me, to your new life of higher consciousness, inner fulfilment, real abundance and happiness. This is where your new life awaits you. Shall we set off together on this journey to discover your path?

Introduction

Our life is like a journey in which, as we advance, the landscape takes a different view from that which is presented at first, and changes again as we become nearer. This is just what happens, especially with our wishes. We often find something else, nay, something better than what we are looking for. Instead of finding as we expected, pleasure, happiness, joy, we get experience, insight, knowledge, a real and permanent blessing, instead of a fleeting and illusionary one. In their search for gold, the alchemists discovered other things - gunpowder, China, medicines, the laws of nature. There is a sense in which, we are all alchemists.
— *ARTHUR SCHOPENHAUER*

ONE
Where am I?

> Every man dies,
> Not every man really lives.
> – *WILLIAM WALLACE*

Have you ever felt lost in this world, like you didn't know where you belong? Have you ever asked yourself, "What am I doing here?" or "Where do I fit into all of this?" Do you ever feel like everyone around you was doing well for themselves? Getting established in their careers, starting a family, having rewarding relationships with their loved ones and family? While you on the other hand, may feel left out from all of this, like a piece to your jigsaw is missing? Do you ever feel like a deluded dog chasing its own tail, or a chicken running around with its head chopped off? Or perhaps a tiny boat, without a rudder, sailing in a rough and stormy sea? Do you feel like you have no destination or any real meaning?

In your everyday life you may go from job to job, relationship to relationship, and at times you may feel disappointment, clinging onto any small moments of happiness for as long as it lasts without any real sense of inner fulfilment. I know how this feels, as I have experienced this in my own life many years ago.

I truly believe that all is about to change for you. I believe you can do anything you want to do as soon as you grasp consciously onto what I'm going to tell you. In this chapter you'll finally understand how this world works and how it operates. And life will start working with you and not against you, in the most rewarding ways.

> If we do not know what port we're steering for,
> no wind is favourable.
> – *LUCIUS SENECA*

EARTH'S CLASSROOM

Welcome to the classroom of life, on planet Earth. You are currently existing in the third dimension of frequency which consists of many resonations of frequencies and consciousness. Depending on how long you attend for, this is where most of your learning will take place. Whilst you draw air into your lungs and your heart pumps blood around your body, you're a student and you'll meet many teachers here.

VIBRATIONS

We are vibrating energy resonating at different frequencies. Some people's energy is dense and slower and other's is faster and lighter. When you get along with someone or feel an attraction to them, you're both resonating at the same frequency. You're literally on the same wavelength. You get their vibes, as we say.

However, when you don't see eye to eye or you just can't connect with some people the frequencies, like magnets don't match up, and you are repelled from one another. Sometimes our frequencies change. In relationships, after a while, one person you were attracted to and loved may have changed their way of thinking, their personality, or even maybe their outlook on life. What happens is their frequency changes as well. Sometimes if we don't accommodate this change or meet them at their level, there is a break-up on a physical and an energetic level. This is the unseen in our lives that controls, changes and manifests on the physical realm. Energetically it is through your consciousness and the raising of frequency to higher awareness and an understanding of who you are, your purpose and meaning which brings about change into your life.

ENERGY VAMPIRES

Have you ever stood next to someone and got a terrible feeling or vibration (or vibe) and your intuition told you to avoid them? Or perhaps you had a conversation with someone who made you feel energetically drained as though they zapped all of your energy and you felt like you had nothing left to give? These people are called energy vampires. They literally suck the energy from you. Sometimes they don't even know what they're doing. Usually their personalities are very needy, insecure and they feel inferior and need reassurance and seek approval.

At the other end of the spectrum there are those that are very enthusiastic, friendly and fun to be around and they motivate you and want you to enjoy yourself, will uplift your spirits and energise you. They will give you energy and build your confidence through their kind words and actions towards you.

PROTECTION FROM ENERGY VAMPIRES

Sometimes it is unavoidable to be around energy vampires. Below are some strategies to help limit being affected by energy vampires.

- Fold your arms as this will place a physical barrier between you and the energy vampire.
- When you're sitting down, cross your ankles. This is another way to block energy being transferred from one person to another.
- If you're on the phone, try and finish the conversation as quickly as possible. You don't have to be rude, but you can be assertive.

These techniques will stop them in their tracks and keep them out of your personal space. Try and avoid these people at all costs, your health and your sanity depend on it.

FEELING GOOD

Remember a time when you felt really good about yourself? When you couldn't put a foot wrong, and you had a good sense of direction and purpose in your life? How did you feel physically at that time? Heavy and lethargic? Light and full of energy and vitality? Yes, that's right, you were feeling lighter and full of energy. That's what it's like when your physical body is vibrating at a higher frequency. Did you also notice at that time that you had great self-esteem, self-worth and confidence? We can all relate to feeling like this at some time in our lives. Did you also notice that your intuition or your gut feeling was correct? And, you could pick up on how your friends and family were feeling? Did you feel more confident in your abilities, stand your ground and speak up for yourself when the moment arose? I'm sure you did.

HIGHER FREQUENCIES

This is what it's like when your body's vibration resonates at a higher frequency. There is more clarity and less chatter going through your mind. When your frequency is high you have more zest and energy to accomplish and achieve old and new projects with ease, as well as achieve a sense of inner fulfilment.

Now you can understand how psychics have trained themselves to raise their vibration levels. They tune into other people's fields of energy, also called the aura or electromagnetic field. This field surrounds our physical body and applies to all living things in this physical reality.

It's exactly like the channels received through television or radio. You first have to tune into and pick up the channel or station you want to receive. There are many different frequencies around you, although you can't see them, they exist. Depending on what frequency you want to tune into and receive this becomes your reality. Whether it is positive or negative, the choice is yours. In your life you always have a decision to make. Positive or negative thoughts, happy or sad feelings, constructive or destructive behaviour? Your choice, your life.

MEDITATION

Psychics also train themselves through the practice of meditation, the calming of their mind. Meditation involves focusing on your breath and letting go of all outside noise to look within. This is how you can raise your vibration and listen to your inner self. Let go of all that 'monkey chatter' in your mind and get a real sense of calm and peace to start living in the now. Meditation is extremely important in connecting with your inner self and allowing you to listen to your intuition, which will be covered in further detail in chapter 10.

POSITIVE BELIEF SYSTEM AND LAW OF ATTRACTION

When you surround yourself with a positive belief system, positive thoughts and positive people you will receive happiness, love and abundance, joy and positive outcomes. When you have negative energy around you, combined with destructive thought patterns and beliefs, you'll surround yourself with the same type of circumstances, and live in fear, being miserable and depressed. How you feel within yourself will manifest itself in your everyday life. This is the law of attraction. We attract to ourselves in our lives, what we think, how we act and ultimately what to expect. Believing it makes it so.

Your thoughts are energy and a higher rate of vibration will always have influence and control over a lower rate of vibration. This is natural law. There are many universal laws here which govern how things work and operate and are unchanging. However, know them, use them and cooperate with them to the best advantage in your life. Throughout this book as we move through the coming chapters, I will let you know about these laws.

It's possible to live with both positive and negative frequencies, but in doing so you'll feel confined and frustrated and your energy will be scattered. It's a better way to live when you're always more positive, confident, loving and enjoying your life. Always expect things to work out for you and in turn you radiate a higher self-worth, self-esteem and work for the greater good for yourself and humankind. Being optimistic should be a way of life for you. If things don't work out as expected, sometimes it can be a blessing in disguise, and at least your mental attitude will be positive.

NEGATIVE ATTITUDES

Don't let a negative attitude and low vibration spoil your life. Being pessimistic will make you feel like life's a struggle, a burden and that's no way to live your life. You want to enjoy your life and be the best that you can be. When your energy is low you'll only ever see the negative in everything and won't be able to look past the storm clouds to see the beauty in the rainbow.

When we feel like this, the body always has a lot more aches and pains, because the flow of energy has become stagnant. So our motivation and desire will be at a low, making you feel unsure and confused and not knowing what direction to take in your life.

When this happens we stop channelling our creativity and imagination and our lives become dull and boring, stagnant and without any direction. All facets of our lives become lifeless and mundane. So what do most people do to increase the energy in their bodies? They eat more, it's called emotional eating, and they devour foods that are high in sugar to give them a boost that they need to get them going. It doesn't have to be foods either, it can be taking up any substance over time which becomes an addiction — caffeine, drugs, alcohol or risky behaviour that gives you a high and makes you escape your reality for a while. People take up these addictions because their inner selves, their souls, aren't being nourished. So they fill up that void of their lives which aren't being met with addictions and self-destructive behaviour. This will be covered in more detail in chapter 11.

HOW THE EARTH CLASSROOM WORKS

And this is how the Earth classroom works. We send out signals of positive or negative frequencies into the energy matrix through our thought patterns, beliefs and attitudes. Whether they are positive or negative, the choice is yours. We get back to us what we send out. As the saying goes, you get back what you put in. Remember your thoughts and beliefs create your reality. It's critical for you to understand this principle.

ENERGY TRANSMITTERS

Ultimately we are energy transmitters and receivers, with the most dominant frequency flowing through our bodies (either positive or negative). The more you become controlled by, and influenced by this state of vibration, you resonate this vibration. This will affect your life depending on your outlook and your thoughts. The higher and more positive the frequency, the better the outcome will manifest in your life, as higher frequencies have more power and influence over slower, negative frequencies. It's a no brainer.

BRINGING BACK POSITIVE ENERGY

You can bring back positive energy into your life with love for yourself, happiness, embracing freedom, finding your path, compassion, good health, strong identity, respect for yourself and the list could go on forever.

INVOLVEMENT IN LIFE STRATEGIES

By bringing back vitality and that love for yourself you have to get involved with life. Start enjoying the things that make you happy and are positive and constructive to your wellbeing. Join a group of people who have similar passions like golf, fishing, cooking, a book club, scrap-booking or walking. These are just a few examples; others include volunteering for your favourite charity for a few hours each week, getting involved in your community and being of service and lending a hand. It not only helps people in need but makes you feel great as well.

When you give back with love and the right intentions you're more likely to receive ten-fold. You will put smiles on the faces of strangers and know you've done your part to contribute something to the community. This will make you feel love, not only for someone else, but yourself as well. It is your service which will give you purpose.

> To do for the world more than the world does
> for you — that is success.
> — HENRY FORD

IMPACT ON THE HUMAN BODY — CHAKRAS

In Hindu and Buddhist tradition and other belief systems, chakras are centres of life force, or vital energy. They correspond to major points in the physical body. The chakras are thought to vitalise the body on a physical, emotional and mental level. Chakras can be described as wheels of light which spin clockwise when open and receiving energy from the life force known as prana, which is universal energy.

They are the main energy generators of our body and are located along the mid-line of our physical bodies. They begin at the base, the root chakra which is red in colour and known as the first chakra. The second chakra also known as the sacral chakra is coloured orange. The third chakra is the solar plexus, which is yellow in colour. The heart chakra is fourth and located at the centre of the chest and coloured green. The fifth chakra is the throat region and coloured sky blue; the sixth is located at the brow also known as the third eye, its colour is indigo. The crown chakra is above the head and is the seventh chakra coloured violet.

SOLAR PLEXUS CHAKRA

The solar plexus (the third chakra) to me is the most important. This corresponds to the mind, the subconscious which is connected to the world within us. When we listen and use our intuition, insight and go with our gut literally (because this is where it's located), we are connected to the intelligence of the universe. This is where the unseen gets manifested into the seen, through our will, our desire to become all that we can be. This centre is all about our personal power and identity.

When we're on our path and we feel good about ourselves we have great self-worth, self-esteem, self-confidence — as you can see its all got to do with self. It's very much about our spiritual development, how you see yourself, taking responsibility for yourself, being accountable and taking the appropriate actions in your daily life to live your life with honour and respect.

CHAKRA PATH

The solar plexus will also let you know if you're on the wrong path because you'll feel uncomfortable in the stomach region. You'll feel sick in the stomach and think, "I don't feel good about this", you may also feel your stomach is in knots. That's your intuition guiding you, warning you physically, letting you know not to go ahead and disrespect yourself. Examples could include going to a job you don't like, or a relationship that isn't working, manipulating people, or doing wrong to someone or something. The solar plexus will let you know.

When you feel nervous, you get butterflies in the stomach, this is your body signalling to you that you're getting worked up and becoming anxious and that you're losing energy. When you're being critical of yourself and others you lose energy from here. Also, if you break your word, you leak energy from this centre as well. When you lose energy you lower your vitality.

Energy vampires take your energy from your solar plexus making you feel depleted. That's why you fold your arms over your stomach which is the location of your solar plexus. Be honourable, keep your personal power, listen to your intuition, and most importantly act on it because it's the gateway to a rich and rewarding life!

CHAKRA CORRELATIONS

As explained earlier, chakras correspond to the colours of the rainbow and they each resonate at a different vibration. They are also connected to major organs within the body as well as the endocrine system. For example, the first chakra corresponds to the testes and ovaries.

I've outlined the main seven chakras but there are many more located throughout the body, for example your hands and feet. The first three chakras correlate to the physical reality, food, survival, sex, creativity, power and relationships, self-worth and identity. The fourth chakra is about love and compassion for oneself and humanity which is also the gateway between the physical reality or vibration and the mystical. That is, what you can't see, but what you can feel. This includes your will, intuition, enlightenment and self-awareness.

It's quite interesting to note that when you're feeling happy and healthy and have heaps of vitality, you wear clothes which suit the way you're feeling and which reflects your mood. These colours will be brighter and more cheerful, whites and blues and pastel colours, as these colours resonate as you guessed it, at a higher vibration, which lifts you up and makes you feel light and happy. When you're down and don't feel great, you will choose to wear darker colours which expresses how you feel, due to a slower vibration and frequency.

It's just like entering a house that has walls painted in bright vibrant colours, they give you energy, put you at ease, make you feel calm and relaxed. Go into a room which is dark and dingy and how do you feel? You guessed it, you feel heavy, lethargic and you are likely to want to get out of there quickly.

CHAKRAS AND THE MUSICAL SCALE

The seven chakras that operate in our bodies also correspond to the seven notes of the diatonic musical scale. At one end of the spectrum there is heavy metal music which can evoke emotions such as anger and aggression, and at the other end of the spectrum there is classical music which can be soft and soothing and evoke a sense of calm.

ANIMALS SENSE ENERGY

Animals can also sense your energy. When you go over a friend's place next or if you have your own pet, take note of their behaviour around you. Observe the cat or dog. See if it will come to you. It may stop, usually two or three feet in front of you depending on how you feel. That's the aura that the animal feels or senses, it will look at you and perhaps wag its tail, bark or meow, depending if it likes your energy and it then may move into your personal space and greet you properly.

AURA

The aura is the electro-magnetic field that surrounds our bodies and is a display of colours outside the physical body. It extends about a metre around and outside the physical body depending on any imbalances in the body which make the aura closer to the body.

HOW TO SEE THE AURA

You can actually focus on looking at someone's aura and seeing the colours that surround their physical body. At first you will see a glow around them and in time, with enough practice you will see colour.

Gifted clairvoyants and intuitive people can tune into someone's aura and tell them what colour is most dominant and also give an indication into how you feel and what's going on in your life.

As I've outlined in this chapter, the chakras, colours, auras and vibrations that we give off provide a better understanding of the reasons why and how we interact with each other in our everyday environments on a more subtle energetic level.

CONSCIOUSNESS

So, not only are we frequencies and vibrations, but we're also consciousness. We're our thoughts, feelings and our experiences — good or bad — which make up our reality. Consciousness is how we perceive our lives either fun, fantastic and a joy to experience and anything in life is possible; or we perceive our life to be a struggle, a burden and everything is too hard, so why bother and give up? It's your decision, your thoughts are energy, be very careful what you think and how you think, because you create your conditions by your beliefs, period. Your life is a reflection from the inside out. You're not separate from your reality, everything you do affects the whole. Treat everything and everyone the way you want to be treated. If you do this, your life will be a beautiful journey, one that you can savour when you look back at it.

Remember, you have a choice in your life of which road to take. Where do you want to focus your energies? Focus them on the now and for a better tomorrow for yourself and those people that you can help today. Start this very moment; get inspired to create something wonderful and magical because life is beautiful.

I know I have been going on about energy and vibration, but I have done this for a reason, because I know there is power in repetition.

Everything on this planet which is alive has energy vibrating through it. The sun creates energy for everything on Earth. Without it, nothing would exist.

I need you to understand that everything is made up of energy, all living things in this physical realm consist of vibration and resonate at a certain frequency. Scientists now believe that everything has an energy signature.

> A human being is part of the whole, called by us 'Universe', a part limited in time and space. He experiences himself, his thoughts and feelings as something separated from the rest – a kind of optical delusion of his consciousness. This delusion is a kind of prison for us, restricting us to our personal desires and to affection for a few persons nearest us. Our task must be to free ourselves from this prison by widening our circles of compassion to embrace all living creatures and the whole of nature in its beauty.
> – ALBERT EINSTEIN

IT'S ALL ABOUT ENERGY

Everything is energy and for you to understand this and become a happier and more fulfilled person and reach the levels of a higher frequency and consciousness, you need to become more spiritually (consciously) aware. You must understand this fact.

To raise your frequency and be at one with your inner self and resonate with cosmic consciousness your illusion will be over and you'll no longer feel separate, but be one with all.

We're energy — our thoughts, what we feel, what we say, what we eat, what we do, our everyday experiences all constitute a form of energy. Our actions and the choices we make, how we feel and react to certain experiences in our lives (whether we let them go or hold onto them) determine the quality and richness of a more fulfilling life, on a day to day basis.

Remember you send out these signals into the matrix of frequencies and vibrations by your thoughts, actions and beliefs. Guess what? It returns to you either the good (positive) or bad (negative) intentions applied. This is how we create our lives. This principle alone has got you where you are today and will change for the better if you choose to change your ways to a more positive mindset.

Have you ever heard sayings such as "you reap what you sow", "what goes around comes around", and my favourite, "wherever attention goes, energy flows"? They all mean the same. You're the captain of your ship, you can sail on into the sunset and live out your dreams or go to no man's land — it's your choice!

The body is a storehouse of memories and emotions and when they become dormant and left unexpressed within our bodies we become physically and spiritually ill. There are many energy medicine practices throughout the world today that can help us unlock these stagnant energies. These include Reiki, crystal therapy, body mind therapy and a discipline called applied or behavioural kinesiology.

KINESIOLOGY

Kinesiology is the link between the body's energy lines (meridians) and the emotions. It is a form of muscle testing. This practice involves a person standing opposite and gets you to hold out your arm straight as you're asked a series of questions. When you respond a negative reaction or response to the questions being asked, the arm being held out is easy to push down by the person providing the emotional, intellectual and physical stimuli. When it's a positive response or a yes, the indicator muscle or arm holds its positive form and stays strong.

So basically, the practitioner talks to the body's consciousness which responds with a yes or no, positive or negative answer. An emotional problem is the result of an unresolved experience from the past, kinesiology can address this connection, and unblock any stagnant energy.

POWER VS FORCE

In David R Hawkins' book *Power VS Force*, he explains:

> Kinesiology is now a well-established science, based on the testing of an all-or-none muscle response stimulus.
>
> The test itself is simple, rapid, and relatively fool-proof: A positive muscle reaction occurs in response to a statement that is obviously true; a negative response occurs if the test subject is presented with a false statement. This phenomenon occurs independently of the test subject's own opinion or knowledge of the topic, and the response has proven cross-culturally valid in any population and consistent over time.
>
> Moreover, we found that this testable phenomenon can be used to calibrate human levels of consciousness so that an arbitrary logarithmic scale of whole numbers emerges. Exhaustive investigation has resulted in a calibrated scale of consciousness, in which the log of whole number from 1 to 1,000 calibrates the degree of power of all possible levels of human awareness.
>
> We see, for instance, that a person in Grief, which calibrates at the low energy level of 75, will be in much better condition if he rises to Anger, which calibrates at 150. If the hopeless can come to want something better (Desire — 125) and then use the energy of Anger at 150 to develop Pride

(175), they may then be able to take the step to Courage, which calibrates at 200, and proceed to improve their individual conditions.

Any meaningful human satisfaction cannot even commence until the level of 250, where some degree of self-confidence begins to emerge as a basis for positive life experiences in the evolution of consciousness.

The mid-200s are associated with semiskilled labor. The high 200s are represented by skilled labor, blue-collar workers, tradesmen, retail commerce and industries. At the level of 300, we find technicians, skilled and advanced craftsman, routine managers, and a more sophisticated business structure. In the mid 300s, we find upper management, artisans, and educators. The 400s are the level of the awakening of the intellect, where true literacy, higher education, the professional class, executives, and scientists can be found.

Just as the level 200 demarcates a critical change of consciousness, 500 is the point at which awareness makes another giant leap. Here, excellence is common in every field of human endeavour, from sport to scientific investigation. A few even make the great leap to the region that calibrates at 600. At this point, an individual's life may become legendary. The signature of the 600s is compassion, pervading all motivation and activity.

Although the levels we have described span a great variation, it's uncommon for people to move from one level to another during their lifetimes. The energy field that is calibrated for an individual at birth only increases, on the average, by about five points.

Nonetheless, it's possible to make sudden positive jumps, leaping up even hundreds of points. If one can truly escape the egocentric draw of sub-200 attractor fields, consciously choosing a friendly, earnest, kind, and forgiving approach to life, and eventually making charity toward others one's primary focus, high levels can certainly be attained.

By becoming more compassionate and loving towards yourself and your fellow humans and expressing how you feel, and the thoughts and actions that you demonstrate on a daily basis, this will put you in a more positive consciously enlightened vibration so your life force (prana) will move freely around your energy body. You will be more creative and more dedicated and motivated to help yourself and to be of service to everyone around you. Now, that's something special you can aim for.

HIDDEN MESSAGES IN WATER

As this chapter draws to a close, a good friend of mine, Lorrie, gave me a book called *The Hidden Messages in Water* by Dr Masaru Emoto. He undertook an experiment where he exposed two jars of mountain spring water to differing stimuli. These included heavy metal music versus classical music, negative versus positive words both written and spoken. The jars of water were then frozen and were examined under a microscope. They were then photographed, revealing the true nature of each jar's water.

This is where the experiment gets fascinating. Depending on what the water was exposed to, the positive stimuli jar of water (classical music, positive words such as love and gratitude) formed beautiful defined crystal structures that looked absolutely amazing. The negative stimuli jar of water (heavy metal music and negative words such as anger and hate) was deformed and distorted within the water molecule form.

Words can be very powerful, they can make us feel happy, sad, offer hope, or make us feel downright miserable. Through our choice of words our intentions can be felt and our desires known. Words can inspire us to move mountains or they can immobilise us with fear. By monitoring the words we use in everyday life, we can instantly change the way we think, feel and live. Throughout your day, monitor the words that you use towards others' in your everyday vocabulary. Avoid words and language such as 'I can't', 'I won't' and 'I'm useless' as they disempower you. Replace them with words such as 'I will', 'I can' and 'I'm good enough' as these words will strengthen and inspire you to become a strong and powerful individual.

> Words form the thread on which we string our experiences.
> – ALDOUS HUXLEY

We're all connected on a vibrational and frequency level and we're all connected to a much higher consciousness in all elements of life's wonders. The frequencies of your thoughts whether they be positive or negative, your good and bad intentions towards people and circumstances and who and what you surround yourself with in your environment, have a major effect on the way you live your life.

Understand our bodies are made up of about 60 percent water. This puts Dr Emoto's research and his findings into a different light (or is that water?!)

So there you have it, I have given you a good understanding on how this classroom called life works, and how we can use our energy, our thoughts, our actions, our attitudes and beliefs to our advantage.

Through these basic principles you will understand that you create your future. You're the director of your movie, you're the master gardener of your soul and you will have a much stronger belief in yourself, you can be happy, live the life that you want for yourself and turn your dreams into a reality, now.

Speaking of dreams, let's go to the next chapter.

> Be dissatisfied with the life you are leading, but when you have rejected it, do not be in despair over yourself... Learn what the wrestling teachers do. Has the boy fallen? "Rise" they say and wrestle again until your strength is renewed. This is how it should be with you. Realise that there is nothing more flexible than the human spirit. It needs but to will and the thing is done, the spirit is set on the right path.
> – EPICTETUS

TWO
Dreams

> If one advances confidently in the direction of his dreams, and endeavours to live the life which he has imagined, he will meet with success unexpected in common hours.
> – HENRY DAVID THOREAU

When we sleep, most of us dream. On average, adults dream between four to six times per night during a stage of sleep called Rapid Eye Movement. We need to listen to our dreams as they're the language of the universe talking to us. If we can understand and decipher the symbology and the interactions of our dreams while we're asleep, we can work out the hidden messages being revealed to us, so we can enjoy and live our true destinies, whilst being awake.

Many great visionaries throughout history had dreams and visions which would change the way we live and interact with one another in our society. Martin Luther King Junior's, "I have a dream" speech was the call for racial equality and to put an end to discrimination in America. His dream came true with Barack Obama becoming the first African American and 44th President to hold office. Dr King's speech gave hope, faith and courage for minorities to pursue and live their dreams not only in the United States, but the world. We need our dreams not only when we're asleep, but also while we're awake and living throughout our daily lives, so we can strive and work towards something fulfilling to reach and live our potential as human beings.

> Some men see things as they are, and say, 'Why?'
> I dream of things that never were, and say, 'Why not?'
> – GEORGE BERNARD SHAW

To truly listen to ourselves we must interpret and analyse the hidden messages our dreams are conveying to us, through symbols, people and places. It can help us identify what we're not consciously aware of as we go about our everyday business. There is no ego or illusion when it comes to the subconscious mind, only truth and insight.

SUBCONSCIOUS MIND

When we aren't listening or picking up on messages and clues through our waking state (consciously) our subconscious mind acts like our silent guide, helping and warning us throughout our daily lives. The subconscious mind also stores our memories of past experiences, feelings, emotions and thoughts which have had a significant impact throughout our lives. Our everyday reality is formed by how we interpret these experiences. If our interpretations are faulty, we become misguided and put limitations on ourselves, which creates negativity and a sense of not being good enough. The subconscious mind is your internal compass guiding you and giving you direction through your gut feelings, inner voice, hunches and by listening to your heart. I constantly tell people to follow their heart as it is never wrong. Your subconscious is like an iceberg. There are two parts to a large iceberg, the top half, which is usually smaller in size, can be seen as the conscious part of you. However, just below the water surface, where the ice is much larger, this is the subconscious mind, which controls and governs our everyday lives.

When you do listen to your heart, it's your subconscious mind which is connected into the universal mind giving you all the information you need to use in your toolbox to overcome any obstacle, fear or challenge you're facing. The subconscious mind is only as good as the beliefs and programs that you have installed into it. If you're running negative beliefs, attitudes and emotions, the subconscious mind will only manifest into your everyday reality what you have put into it, through your conscious thoughts.

To lead you down the path of self-discovery and inner knowing you must be awake to the fact there is a force in the universe, which is so powerful, everything you need to know is available to you at any given moment. Your questions will be answered, when you ask. All you need to do is listen.

> The power to move the world is in your subconscious mind.
> – WILLIAM JAMES

UNIVERSAL MIND

The universal mind is the connection that we have with the unseen world around us. By listening to yourself and following your heart you're tapping into the universal supply of all knowing. It is when you act on the directions of the universal mind, which is connected to your subconscious mind, that you manifest your dreams into a reality by the law of cause and effect. Through your actions you will create your world around you.

If you don't listen to your subconscious mind, it will try and get messages through to you via your dreams and sometimes through the use of symbols in your dreams. As these are all clues for you to analyse and decipher. When I talk about symbols, I mean the people, places, events and actions of what is taking place in your dreams.

DREAM EXAMPLES AND ANALYSIS

Take this dream for example. You're driving too fast in your car, you take the bend too wide, skid into a fence and are badly injured. I would interpret this dream as you need to slow your life down and start taking control of some aspect of your life. Whether it be your relationship, lifestyle, work or some other part of your life, you're overdoing it.

A recent dream follows: I was swimming at the beach and I got caught in a rip and started to struggle. A stranger asked if I needed help to which I replied that I was ok. I was not ok, and a few minutes later, I'm a long way off shore, although I eventually made it back to the shore exhausted. The same stranger appeared again and said in future, when someone offers help, let them, don't be afraid to ask for help. I got the message loud and clear. Anyone who knows me could tell you I don't like to ask for help or put anyone out. However, I'm working on this and now, especially while working on this book, I've had to ask for help and rely on others. My life has become easier because I am listening to my dreams.

I have always listened to my dreams throughout my life and sometimes when I don't understand or can't decipher the dream, it will keep occurring, until I pick up on the message which is being conveyed to me. When I pick up the message, I can live a much happier and more balanced lifestyle which improves my overall outlook on life.

I'm sure there are some of you who are saying right now, "Oh, I don't dream when I sleep or I can't remember my dreams." Well, everybody dreams at least several times a night when we experience rapid eye movement, a state we're in while sleeping.

DREAMING IS NATURAL

Dreaming is a natural state when we fall asleep and depends on what you're doing throughout the day. If your life is hectic and you're really busy and stressed, you'll find your dreams are more frequent and the colours, people and places are more vivid and intense than usual, making you recuperate and recover, for the day ahead.

I find I always dream more when I'm relaxed and in tune with myself and have absorbed energy from places of nature, such as the beach or the rainforest, where the location's vibrations are of a higher frequency. These places are untouched by human-made infrastructure which increases the frequency. Human-made infrastructure has a lower frequency and therefore messages and signals get criss-crossed and distorted.

Do you find it hard to relax and have peace of mind in the city — with all the tall buildings, traffic and the hustle and bustle of everyday life, with computers, telephones and electricity all around you? You tend to hurry, doing five things at once. You have much mind chatter going on causing you to be stressed out. This environment vibration is of a low frequency and stops you from tuning in and listening to yourself.

NATURE HELPS DREAMING

Getting back to nature is very healing and therapeutic for your soul. These places do wonders to calm you, lift the frequency of your body and calm and still your mind. This allows you to tap into the universal mind and receive your visions, ideas and provide the answers to all you need to know about making your dreams come true.

EXERCISE – DREAM STRATEGIES

Now if you can't remember your dreams, I would like you to do these four things for me:

1. Buy some Howlite crystals, these ancient stones will help aid you in remembering your dreams upon awakening. Place them on your bedside table or somewhere close to where you sleep.
2. Buy a small notepad and pen to place by your bedside table. During the night or upon rising in the morning you can write

down your dreams. Jot it down while the dream is still fresh in your mind and before you forget.
3. Buy a dream dictionary or download an app, it doesn't have to be a fancy one. Just a reference guide until you can interpret your dreams on your own.
4. As you are preparing for sleep, say to yourself aloud or in your mind, "When I wake up I will remember my dreams". By doing this, you are planting a seed and giving your subconscious mind a direct order that you want it to help you remember your dreams when you wake up.

BE PERSISTENT

I must point out, it's very important you understand, if after using the strategies above for a few days or weeks and you still can't recall your dreams in the morning, that's ok. Don't quit, don't give up, give it time. It takes practice and time to change and getting into a new habit and routine of remembering your dreams. It's just like going to the gym and getting fit, it takes time. Have patience, and have fun with it as well.

Enjoy this part of your life, as we spend about a third of our life asleep. Why not let your dreams serve you, so you can draw inspiration, insight and guidance from your night travelling adventures?

> Energy and persistence conquer all things.
> – BENJAMIN FRANKLIN

FUTURE DREAMS

Now I want to ask you about your dreams, while you're awake. You know, the ones you had envisioned for yourself when you were a child growing up.

For me, I wanted to have my own successful business helping people with their lives. All the while, making a difference in the society in which I live. There's nothing more fulfilling than seeing your dreams coming true, as you will find out.

So what was your dream? Now I want you to think back, before anybody told you that you're not clever enough, it will never work, it's too risky, it will be impossible for you to do that, you can't make money from that. You know, the dream squashers. Maybe it was your parents, siblings, teachers or friends or just peer group pressure. You have to ask yourself what have they done, are they living their dreams? You'll find most of them are not, but the people who are, will encourage you to go for it and live the life you want to live.

I went through a stage like this in my life when I was just about to start my own business. I came across people in my life who said things such as, "It will never work; people won't want to visit your home; you're not good enough; you won't make enough money to make a living; you're crazy."

However, I believed in my dream which was to successfully earn a living, work the hours that I wanted and to have the freedom to have a day off and go on holiday when I wanted to, as well as be my own boss. Sounds great doesn't it? Well it is — and you can do it too!

BELIEVE IN YOUR DREAMS

Your dreams are yours — don't let anyone ever take them away from you, they're yours to be lived out. Become limitless — the only limitations we have are the ones we place on ourselves. Don't listen to the negative nancies, there are many of them. You'll find they're still working in the jobs they don't like, with a set amount of money the organisation in which they work is willing to pay them, for a boss they probably dislike. Not in all cases, but something of this nature. Don't let anyone discourage you from living your dreams. This is your life, enjoy it!

> The greatest achievement was at first and at a time a dream. The oak sleeps in the acorn; the bird waits in the egg; and in the highest vision of the soul a waiting angel stirs. Dreams are like the seedlings of realities.
> — JAMES ALLEN

CHILDHOOD DREAMS

I ask you this question. What were your dreams as a child? When we're at a young age, we're still in spirit and haven't been affected by society, been programmed to think and feel and behave a certain way, indoctrinated by the education system instead of thinking for ourselves and pushed to learn certain topics which hold no interest or value to us.

The pressure of everyday life eventually catches up with you, and you're caught and fed into the machine of mediocrity and the status quo. You need to still believe that life is an adventure and fun and you can enjoy life and be paid for something you love doing and have the freedom to do what you want.

You see, when you're young you listen to your heart a lot more as your mind isn't as busy or noisy. No expectations have been placed upon you, so you can listen to your soul talking to you, giving you direction, guidance and insight into what you need to do.

It's time to make the commitment to change your life for today. When you decide to take action to live your dreams, the universe will guide you to your path through a number of ways. These can include a message from a stranger, an idea or impulse that comes to you, or through a thought or feeling. This will lead you to fulfil your dreams.

> Concerning all acts of initiative and creations there is one elementary truth – that the moment one definitely commits oneself, then providence moves, too.
> – JOHANN WOLFGANG VON GOETHE

MEDITATION IN THE NOW

Our dreams and great visions come when we are in a state of meditation, when the mind is still, even now, and at any age. This is where we get our best ideas, imagination and creativity is flowing and we're in the moment not focusing on anything else but what we're doing. It's being in the now. You don't have to be in Tibet, in a cave chanting mantras or sitting in the lotus position. This state can be achieved at anytime whether you're washing up, fishing, playing with the children, in the shower, or outside on the balcony having a cup of tea.

DREAMS MADE MANIFEST

Take a look around you right now. The appliances that you have in your home or at work and use daily such as the refrigerator, microwave, toaster, computer, oven, stereo system, smart phone — they all began with someone's dream, a vision they had. In that moment of silence they had an idea, acted on that idea and turned it into a reality, that was their dream.

Take a look outside now, do you see the car parked in the driveway or on the street? Look up in the sky, do you see a plane or helicopter? These are all dreams that were manifested into reality. The people who came up with these inventions or dreamt to be a pioneer, were everyday people like you and me. They tapped into the universal mind, believed in their ideas and visions, had the courage, determination and discipline to follow through with their dreams and not let anyone persuade them otherwise. They decided to take action and by having faith in themselves, a desire and a strong expectation to succeed they knew the outcome would be victorious! Defeat and surrender was not in their creed. I believe you're good enough and worthy enough to live out your dreams. Do you?

> Whatever course you decide upon, there is always someone to tell you that you are wrong. There are always difficulties arising which tempt you to believe that your critics are right. To map out a course of action and follow it to an end requires courage.
> – RALPH WALDO EMERSON

When your mind is still you're in the moment and time is passing you by very quickly, at this moment we are experiencing flow. You're responding at this time to live, not resisting, you're going with the flow, enjoying the activity that you're doing and becoming one with it. It's a beautiful experience to have and it's yours for the taking. Do you want to live your life like this?

This is how your dreams and visions come to you, at these moments when you least expect it. Your soul will talk to you, you're open at this time to receive messages and omens, your channels are ready to broadcast to you, your dreams and great visions for your future. Let your dreams enhance your possibilities, inspire and motivate you. When you listen and absorb these messages, creativity will follow.

> He who lives in harmony with himself, lives in harmony with the universe.
> – MARCUS AURELIUS

GOODBYE EXCUSES

If you're saying right now, "I'm too old; I have no time; I'm too busy; I have too much responsibility with my family" these are all excuses. Goodbye excuses, if you want change you must change first. It's time to create balance in your life, time to let creativity flow into your life and reconnect with the universal intelligence. Let it send you the ideas and insights you need to change your life. Be quiet, still and listen.

There's an old Zen proverb, "The bow forever taut will break." Get back to enjoying your life. Life is not stressful, only the stressful thoughts that you choose to think. Love your life, love yourself, nurture yourself, and give time to yourself, it's time to become creative. Don't you think it's time to wake up and smell the roses? There's more freedom in being happy and enjoying your life, when you feel like this, you believe you can do anything, the possibilities and opportunities are everywhere. The best thing about life is we can start and begin our dreams now, the only thing that is stopping you is you. Don't be your own worst enemy. It's time to play an active role in your dreams, no longer a bystander sitting on the sidelines of life. Where has this taken you so far?

Put your ideas and insights down onto a piece of paper, start your plans of action. When you do this you are showing your intentions to the universe that you are ready to turn your dreams into a reality.

Have the perseverance, strength and courage to follow through and go for it. You won't regret you did. Become a life artist, create the life you want for yourself. Believe in yourself and encourage yourself, because when you do magic happens.

The only regret is the chance or missed opportunity never acted on. Fear is temporary, regret forever. Begin it now, life is too short, listen to yourself, live your dreams. No more excuses.

The future belongs to those who believe in the beauty of their dreams.
– ELEANOR ROOSEVELT

THREE
Tomorrow land

> We are very near to greatness; one step and we are safe; can we not take the leap?
> — RALPH WALDO EMERSON

When the majority of people aren't living their dream or aren't working towards obtaining their visions for their future, they will often visit tomorrow land. Although it is a funny name it does exist, and it's open for business and free to stay, but it does come at a cost to you, your happiness and your inner fulfilment. Some people go their whole lives visiting and use every excuse under the sun to put off their plans for today and for their future and making their dreams come true. Tomorrow land is where you neglect, for another day, the ideal lifestyle, your dreams and the life you want to live.

PROCRASTINATION

I must also tell you that someday, another day, and one day, aren't days of the week and that procrastination is like a disease that eats away at our self-esteem, self-worth, self-confidence and our precious moments. You know deep down that you're not trying hard enough in your life to live the life that you want and you're paying the price for it because maybe you are unhappy with the job you're in, and the relationship you're in is not working for you, or maybe you don't have the freedom to do what you like, when you like. But, this can all change when you understand you can do anything you put your heart into. It's that simple.

DO IT TODAY

"I'll do it tomorrow!", "I know I should be doing that, but not now", "I'll give my partner one more chance, I know it will get better". Does this sound like somebody you know? Welcome to the delusional soul, it's time to wake up! It's time to say, "Today is the day I let go of this destructive behaviour and draw all my strength and willpower back into the now". It's time for you to become a doer. Don't say one day, that day will never come.

Once you realise that procrastination needs to be dealt head on, the sooner you begin the tasks you set for yourself, and the easier and more enjoyable life begins to flow for you.

> The present moment is a powerful goddess.
> – JOHANN WOLFGANG VON GOETHE

ROUTINE OF BEGINNING

When you get into this routine of beginning and not delaying, the easier it is for you to say yes to life and to become what you want to be and set yourself on the path to complete whatever is put in front of you. The more confident you become in yourself, you will feel a new sense of accomplishment and you then realise you can do anything you want. You begin to believe the incredible and achieve the impossible.

The longer we hold onto tasks and jobs that need to be started and completed, the longer life tends to be held in limbo for us. Perhaps you don't want to begin due to emotional handicaps such as fear, anxiety or worry. These emotions keep you on the sidelines of life meaning the longer your unhappiness and your desired life will be out of reach.

We do things in our lives out of either pain or pleasure. This is the force that drives our habits and behaviours and controls our lives. Sometimes circumstance forces us to finally take action in getting done what we have to do, as the consequences are too painful.

When you procrastinate the energy around you begins to slow down and you feel stagnant, lost and confused. Basically you feel like your life and the reasons you're in it, have shut down. Do you know what this feels like?

> A man who suffers before it is necessary, suffers more than is necessary.
> – SENECA

You have to ask yourself, "Is living in tomorrow land healthy for me?", "Does it make me feel like I'm being productive with my life?", "Do I need to muster up all the energy and determination in the world to begin the smallest of tasks?"

Another place exists, however, here you can live the life you want, you're happy and healthy, you work in a job you like and your relationships with your partner, family and friends are authentic. In this positive place you have a sense of inner fulfilment in your life and you know that you can accomplish anything you put your heart into.

FREEDOM TOWN

Welcome to freedom town. To get to freedom town you must overcome all your fears and your past programming by society and culture. Believe you're good enough, believe in yourself and that you can do anything you set your heart on, to live a life worth living. You need to leave tomorrow land behind for good.

If any of these ring true for you, I'm glad you have this book as it demonstrates that you're actively working towards changing procrastination into action and wanting to move forward in your life.

When you think about how long you have stayed in this routine of procrastination and not doing what you need to do in order to live the life you want, does it make you angry, frustrated or filled with self-pity? If you feel like this and you can recognise and feel these emotions, this is a good sign. It shows that you're ready and willing to move forward in your life. Your emotions will motivate you into action and when you act, new beginnings occur, bringing a sense of a renewed life.

STRATEGIES

Below is a list of strategies to set you on the path to freedom town. You will need a note book and pen to get started.

- Begin to acknowledge how you feel. Keep a journal to let those feelings and thoughts out, express them by writing them down and let them go.
- Ask yourself the question, "How will I feel if I don't do this task?"
- Will doing this task give me more meaning, pleasure and inner fulfilment? Whenever you feel yourself falling back into the trap of putting things off you can draw on this thought to push you forward.
- Keep a list of things you aim to achieve each day and cross them off as they are accomplished.
- If you were unable to achieve every task on your list ask yourself, "What could I have done to achieve one thing that I put off?"
- Carry over the remaining tasks for your list for tomorrow and prioritise them in the order you want to achieve them.

- Put a timeframe on each task of approximately how long you think it will take for you to achieve the task during the day.
- To make it easier on yourself, set aside time slots during the day to work on your tasks to push through procrastination.
- Put a time limit on your task/project so you've got nowhere to hide. Your friends or colleagues will ask you how you're going and you can give them an honest answer. I used this tactic for the completion of this book — it works!
- Once you put yourself into the now and you finish one of the assigned tasks ask, "Was that so bad?" How do you feel about yourself? You feel great? Productive? That's excellent. Crossing tasks off your list can be satisfying.
- Another way to get your jobs completed in a certain time and stop procrastination in its tracks is to tell people what you're doing and when you'll be finished. It will help you become accountable and to take responsibility for your tasks.

A good way to know if you're procrastinating throughout the day is to look back at your list and ask yourself if you used your time effectively today? Or, did you squander your time and waste another day of your life?

> We have time enough, if we will but use it aright.
> – JOHANN WOLFGANG VON GOETHE

TIME CONSCIOUS

Make your time work for you by prioritising what is really important to you. Learn how to be conscious of how you're spending your time throughout the day, and meeting your priorities at the appropriate times. Manipulate time so it works for you, not against you. Time does fly by, but understand you're the pilot. You have complete control of the actions and choices you make, so enjoy the journey and the path that you travel. The destination will be all the more fulfilling.

Please don't tell me you have no time to get things done and that you're too busy throughout your day, these are excuses and if something as important as helping you change your life isn't important enough, I don't know what is. Everybody, at some point in their day has time to prioritise their most important tasks. It should be at a time when energy is high, but it must be done at some point, that's the key.

We all have time but we must prioritise our time. This is how we get things accomplished and achieved in our lives. The days soon turn into weeks, which turn into months, and months into years. Then you can look back at your life and say either, "I've wasted another year of my life and my dreams and ambitions have fallen by the wayside", or "I have done so much this year, I've accomplished this, and this, I feel great about myself and feel like I can do anything, my future looks bright." I know personally which one I would rather be saying and it's definitely the latter.

> The great dividing line between success and failure can be expressed in five words, "I did not have time."
> — ANONYMOUS

Everything in your life always begins with you. As soon as you start working on your dreams and your 'to do' lists, the sooner the doors of opportunity will be opened up for you. With this comes a new found energy and vitality which will make you excited about getting involved with life again. Inspiration is now a part of your life. You will no longer say "I'm bored", because your moments now are filled full of activity which you have chosen to do. Boredom is procrastination in action. Your life's moments are no longer wasteful. Bums on seats now rule the day. You no longer have the time to escape from activities which need to be done. It's time to make the decision to live in the moment and ask yourself what do I need to do now, to start the tasks I have set myself? Sit down (bums on seats) and begin, and it will eliminate all of this anxiety which as been looming over you like a dark cloud. You're now in the moment and your undivided attention is on your current activity. That wasn't so bad was it?

Would you rather be in a state of anxiety and fear for putting off things in your life and living like this all the time? You deserve better than this, I believe, don't you?

DAYDREAMING

Let go of daydreaming which is counterproductive to what you want to accomplish here. Daydreaming will drain your energy and make you feel empty inside. It's your imagination which is a constructive thought, the beginning of something new when placed in the hands of a doer — which is you. All dreams will materialise right before your very eyes, when you decide to act.

By getting into a good routine of living in the moment, boredom will be a thing of the past, you'll be productive and satisfied that you can accomplish anything you put your mind to. Now you know you can do this, what is it that you really want? It's time to look at your goals. Let's get serious.

> In every enterprise, consider where you would come out.
> – PUBLIUS SYRUS

GOALS

It's time to direct your energy, focus and fill that void within yourself to bring direction into your life. Make the decision now before it's too late, otherwise you have no control of your life's outcome. It's time to challenge yourself, raise the bar, believe in your abilities and let go of doubts and worries and transform yourself to be the person you want to be. Your goal is to make you feel good about yourself in the now. Make sure your goals are interesting and important to you. When you choose your goals be honest with yourself and ensure they express who you are and not just to impress others.

By writing down all your goals and setting a plan of action you will create momentum and desire to attain all you wish to achieve which will give you the sense of tremendous accomplishment.

> We must cultivate our garden.
> – VOLTAIRE

STRATEGIES TO ACHIEVE EVERYTHING YOU WANT FROM LIFE

As I've explained, you can achieve anything and everything you want from life, you just need to make a start. **To begin, write down all your goals.**

- Goals can be small, large, short-term, or long-term — they should include everything you want to achieve for yourself. These are lifetime goals.
- You can brainstorm and continually refine your goals until you are happy with your list.
- Once you think you've included everything you want from your life, try to break them up into categories.

- Categories can include relationships, career, financial, education, hobbies or artistic endeavours, health and community. These just provide an overview, you will know from your list of goals the categories that apply.

I don't care how crazy you think this is, the possibilities and opportunities in life are endless and if you can believe it, you can achieve it. Remember it's time to engage in taking more risks, climbing the tree of success, going out onto the end branch and picking the beautiful fruit for your liking. It's there for the picking. Raise the bar on yourself and get ready to grow in confidence and be all that you can be.

The next step is writing a plan of action. Now that you have your list of what you want to achieve, you can break it down into smaller goals which outline how you can achieve your goals.

The following list will help you formulate your plan of action.

- Ask yourself, "How are you going to get to where you need?"
- Who can help you?
- Who else has achieved what you want for yourself?
- There is so much information at your fingertips today, you just need to look. Do some research — online, pick up the phone, or even your local library.
- Talk to like-minded people, you will be very surprised by how people will help when you ask. Start with questions such as how they got to where they are, and how they achieved their success and happiness. If it's appropriate you could ask them to be a mentor.
- There are helpful people everywhere just waiting to help you. Identify the people, community groups, chambers of commerce etc who can help put you on your path.
- Set clear and specific goals and make them realistic.
- Motivate yourself and place importance on your goals, focus your attention.
- Become determined to reach your goals which will only harness a great experience for you and keep you motivated in achieving a favourable outcome.
- List any obstacles or speed bumps which you may have

to overcome along the way to achieve your goals, it could be going back to night school or getting a qualification or other work experience. Don't get disgruntled, relax and let go, don't react but respond in a positive manner to your challenges along the way. They call this adversity, these obstacles and roadblocks are put there to test you and make you grow.
- Put a timeframe on the smaller tasks, do them first and work on the larger ones slowly. Don't do a half-hearted job.
- Remember when thinking about and writing down the goals you want to achieve for yourself, make sure that you raise the bar on yourself, so that your goals aren't so easy to obtain. So you can push yourself and test yourself to discover you have so much more hidden potential than you realise, giving you the encouragement and the esteem to make you understand you can do anything your heart desires, if you're willing to put the effort in.
- When you feel discouraged, look forward for the end result. Ask yourself, "What's in it for me, what am I getting out of this?"
- Visualise yourself with all your goals completed and how happy you will be.
- Act like you're a winner now that everything and everyone is working to help you achieve your goals.
- Be positive and let the flow of creativity channel into your life like an endless stream of water flowing into an abundant sea of opportunity.

By undertaking these steps you'll find that the bright light of ambition and dedication will be strong within you. We need a desire to get up in the morning knowing we are working for a brighter future for ourselves, our family and the wider community as a whole. Once we get the ball rolling it's hard for energy to stop, remember wherever focus goes, energy flows. Momentum is crucial to keep the ball rolling in any endeavour you want to participate in, to see it through to completion.

MOTIVATION

In turn, you can understand you're actively contributing to your life in a positive way. There is power in motivation and action and commitment will keep you going until you have finished. All it takes is persistence which is such a valuable trait to have, being persistent is what will keep you going a little bit each day, day after day, while all the others drop off and give up. This is a true sign of a winner and as Winston Churchill said, "Never, never, never give up." The winning formula to get you from tomorrow land to freedom town is **positive action plus persistence and commitment = accomplishment.** Procrastination is no longer in your vocabulary, those days are gone. You, my friend are now an achiever.

When you put effort into your life this will bring about change for a better tomorrow and when you feel and see change there is growth for you as a person and in turn your potential becomes infinite.

You'll be excited to wake up in the morning, another day to be all that you can be and when there's excitement there's activity and in turn this will bring accomplishment knocking at your very door. A new sense of freedom and joy will touch your very soul.

There must be great intentions in following your dreams and accomplishing everything you want to do in your life. Don't just do things for money, prestige or popularity as this is all ego based and will keep you connected to superficial needs and wants. There is a much bigger picture than this. Enjoy and love what you do, help people, be of service to everyone, be authentic and genuine and live life for a higher purpose.

BEING AUTHENTIC

The foundations for a balanced, successful and happy life are to be authentic, genuine, honest and have good values and morals, integrity, faith, love for yourself and others and understand we are all in this life to love and be of service.

My intentions for you and I for the future are positive. Just like your actions and effort put into purchasing this book are of a positive nature. In turn it will bring about a positive change in your life and you will be illuminated and enlightened when reading this book.

DISCOVER YOUR TALENTS AND ABILITIES

Understand how blessed you are to have talents and abilities which have been given to you and only you, to serve out a higher purpose here. Your talents and abilities are like water in the ground, the water needs to be brought to the surface so it can be of use to you and everybody else. Just like your talents, strengths and abilities, they need to come out of you and brought forward.

Just like the water drawn out of the ground, then it needs to be brought to the market place so it can be used and shared among society. Without taking your talents and abilities to the marketplace and providing a service to everybody, your gifts are going to waste and die inside of you.

Your gifts are to be used to make your community a better place. When you do this you'll find and recognise that giving is better than receiving. This proverb sums it up, "If you give a rose, the scent will remain on your hands forever". True happiness in life comes from giving. Try it for yourself and see the true connection you make with people, no external riches will ever give you this inner fulfilment. It's one of life's many blessings. Be of service and share your gifts and talents with the world.

Genetically we are all different and everyone is gifted and unique in their own special way. I am encouraging you to discover and awaken your talents and abilities, and in turn, be of service and value to society. Make where you live a pleasure for yourself and all of those around you. This is love in action.

LIVE YOUR LIFE

To enjoy your life you must live life not just exist, there's a difference. Life's like a bucket what you put into it is what you get out of it. There's no tomorrow, only today. When you work on yourself today, you create for yourself a better tomorrow.

> A tree that can fill the span of a man's arm, grows from a downy tip,
> A terrace nine storeys high rises from handfuls of earth,
> A journey of a thousand miles starts from beneath one's feet.
> – *LAO-TZU*

I am forever telling people this every day of my life: Don't think so much…Just do!

> There is but one cause of human failure and
> this man's lack of faith in his true self.
> – *WILLIAM JAMES*

Discover Your Path

There is a Chinese proverb that states, "All troubles start with the mouth!" Most people talk about what they're going to do, but don't action it or follow through with it, which becomes quite embarrassing for them. Especially if you ask if they have started what they set out to do. There's another Zen proverb, "There are three things you can never get back — a shot arrow, the spoken word and a missed opportunity." Every moment is precious and can't be taken back. Seize the day, turn thought into action, action into reality.

Always stick by your word in life and in return you will be respected and admired for being a person of your word. With this comes the inner gift of self-worth, and inner confidence. A person who stays true to their word is honest, trustworthy and has integrity.

Begin your life now not tomorrow, otherwise it may never come. As Mark Twain says, "At the end of your life you will be more disappointed by the things you didn't do, than the ones you did do." Start your book before it materialises, ask that someone special on a date, start that college course to get you the career you want. Become active in your life, lose weight now, have better relationships with your family and friends, be kinder and love yourself more, start travelling and see your special destination, board an aeroplane for the first time. It's all yours for the taking, what have you got to lose?

Are you ready to pack your bags and head off to freedom town and say goodbye to tomorrow land forever?

Okay then…Don't think, do…begin it now and watch your life change because guess what, you've decided it's time. If nothing changes, nothing changes. You can do it! I believe in you!

> To be what we are, and to become what we are capable of becoming, is the only aim of life.
> – BARUCH SPINOZA

FOUR

The past...
Stop going back there

Do not dwell in the past
Do not dream of the future
Concentrate the mind on the present moment.
— BUDDHA

Although the past is no longer here many of you may still hold onto the past like an old companion who walks around with you wherever you go, defiant in keeping your attention unshakeable.

Whether an experience happened a second ago or twenty years ago it can still be fresh in your mind which keeps you trapped like in a time machine.

Stop allowing the program of your past to control you. You can change your beliefs, actions and emotions and be in charge of the direction of your life.

DON'T DIG UP THE PAST

The reason I've devoted a chapter to address the topic of the past is because so many people continue to go back into the past, digging up old graves, and remembering times past. Whether it is issues with family or school and perhaps how you were treated, or even how your last relationship ended, the past can bring up negative emotions which are detrimental to your wellbeing.

These emotions give you low self-esteem, limited self-worth and a feeling that you have no sense of control over your life. Stop feeding your worry, anxiety and fear energy. If you're doing this, you're losing energy in the now and stopping yourself from being aware in the present.

What's past is prologue.
— SHAKESPEARE

STOP REHEARSING YOUR UNHAPPINESS

A large majority of people use the past to keep themselves stuck until they wake up and discover life is passing them by and they need to move on and take stock of their life. You need to stop rehearsing your unhappiness and unsatisfying past. Don't concern yourself with justifying your misery. It's time to stop being a slave to your past and make the most of what's in front of you, today, now.

> We try to make virtues of the faults we have to wish to correct.
> — LA ROCHEFOUCAULD

DON'T PLAY THE VICTIM

By keeping yourself trapped in the past, you are playing the victim and this gives what you think is an excuse to sit on the sidelines of life and not take responsibility for yourself, or let someone else have control over you. It's more comfortable this way to do nothing and disempower yourself.

Have you ever met someone at a social gathering and downloaded your personal history so they would feel sorry for you, or so they would take it easy on you or be friendlier towards you?

Maybe you had a bad childhood or your parents got divorced at an early age, had family problems, or haven't spoken to your parents for many years. These are all control dramas which keep you locked in a box and labelled. It's time to stop disempowering yourself.

People use these excuses like they're using imaginary powers over others, usually for self-pity. Unfortunately people who do this are hurting themselves because sooner or later people wise up and get sick of hearing about it and move onto greener pastures because it's too painful to listen to and draining to deal with. It's time to change the channel folks and paint a new self-portrait as this one's too gloomy and depressing.

For some, it's much easier to live in the past and play the victim than to actually live in the now and get on with their lives, move forward and work on themselves today for a happier and joyous life.

Until you decide to let go of the past, move on and learn from what has happened, your growth and development will be at a standstill.

> It is dangerous to abandon oneself to the luxury of grief, for it deprives one of courage and even the wish for recovery.
> – HENRI FREDERIC AMIEL

LET GO OF PERSONAL BAGGAGE

You must let go of all your personal baggage that keeps you stuck in the past. You must have enough energy now so you have the ability to move in the direction of a better life.

Dr Wayne Dyer uses this great analogy of how the majority of people believe the past drives their future. The stern is the back of the boat and the wake is the trail left behind the boat as the boat sails forward. Now ask yourself this question, "Can a trail behind the boat make the boat go forward?" No! Of course it can't.

So why do the majority of people live in the illusion that it does? Now understand the boat is you and the wake is your past, does your past get played over and over in your mind? This is where you lose all your energy and vitality every day. Does it make you move forward like a boat? Of course it doesn't. It traps you, and gets you stuck like you've got an anchor attached to the bottom of the ocean.

It's time to let go of your personal baggage, which drains you, and like that anchor it keeps you miserable and stagnant and stationary, just like your life. It's time to pull up anchor, be free, set sail and move forward — don't you think?

> To reach a port we must sail –
> Sail, not tie at anchor
> Sail, not drift.
> – FRANKLIN D. ROOSEVELT

How can growth and change come into your life if you won't let go of your past and make space for today? Until you decide the past no longer has a purpose, apart from learning from it, and you finally realise that it's an unhealthy way to live, you won't progress to bring about change and growth. Don't you think it's time you escaped your mental prison called your past?

THROW OUT THE OLD COAT OF THE PAST

I understand you have a past, we all do. This chapter has been written for all those who wear the past like an old coat that they just can't throw out. Until you throw away the old coat and the shackles that keep your energy stagnant and back in times gone by, you won't be able to have enough focus, energy, awareness and vitality to bring about freedom and abundance for today, now.

> Confine yourself to the present.
> – MARCUS AURELIUS

THE TWO MONKS

I would like to share a Buddhist parable about a couple of monks who are on their way to a temple to meditate for the morning.

> Two Buddhist monks come to a creek crossing where they find a little old, frail lady who is upset about not being able to cross the creek to pray. The older of the two monks offers to carry her across. The old lady thanks him so much for his kindness.
>
> The young monk is standing there with his mouth open, astounded at the older monk's behaviour and actions. After the older monk has placed the lady on the other side of the creek and they have said their goodbyes, they continue on their journey. The younger monk is silent and in disbelief at what he just witnessed.
>
> During the last five kilometres of their walk he asks the older monk, "We took vows not to touch a woman, how could you carry the old lady across the creek?" The older monk replies, "You saw how I carried her across the creek and put her down, how come you have carried this thought for the last five kilometres and haven't put her down?"

By being tolerant and putting yourself in other people's shoes you leave a lot more room in your life and leave space for the now. When it's time to put the past down, put it down and move on. The past is the past and that's where it should stay. The past no longer exists in fact, it has never existed it's actually an abstract concept in our minds. Remember time is a human-made concept which we have virtually made into our realities. It's an illusion because when you think about it, the only time we have is right now. Not yesterday, not tomorrow, not next week, but now, and the sooner you understand that the only time is now, you'll appreciate this moment is all we have.

When you grasp what I'm talking about your time becomes very precious all of a sudden and you won't waste it on frivolous activities and complaining. It's time to stop playing with your emotional and mental wounds, let them heal and let go.

FOCUS ON THE MOMENT

Begin to put all your focus and attention into the moment that you have and watch your life move forward. Some strategies to help you do this are listed below.

- Be consciously aware of how many times you think about the past for whatever reason throughout the day.
- Become aware of your destructive behaviour and thoughts throughout the day. Make a list so you can monitor how often your energy gets sucked back into the past.
- Once you realise how often you are doing this, make a conscious effort to get back into the moment by saying to yourself, "Stop". The sooner you can begin to stop it dead in its tracks you can become more constructive with your time and energy.

WHAT ARE YOU DOING WITH YOUR LIFE?

Ask yourself these questions to assess your life direction, and to identify how the past may be impacting you in the now.

- How do you feel about yourself?
- Are you paralysed by the past?
- Are you not able to move forward?
- Do you feel miserable and sorry for yourself?
- Are you excited about waking up each day, taking life as it comes, going with the flow and enjoying your journey and not the destination?
- Do you feel you need to make amends with members of your family over old grievances?
- Have you started your 'to do' lists of things you'd like to achieve for the future?
- Are you studying to better your financial and career prospects?
- How is your health? Have you started a healthy eating plan to lose or gain weight?

TAKE FULL RESPONSIBILITY

Become consciously aware right now and take full responsibility for your life. Become the person you want to be. Through action and effort you will start to achieve, opportunities will begin to present themselves and when they do grab them with both hands. The more positive you are, the more energy and vitality you will have to tackle whatever life puts in your way. To me, this is the only way to live and I know you want this for yourself.

STRATEGIES TO LET GO OF THE PAST

Below are some simple strategies to help you identify past issues or regrets that may be holding you back.

- If you feel to bring up the past is the best way to let go of it, start by remembering those experiences that keep you buried there.
- Talk them through with a friend. Be honest, open and accountable. Ask your friend to just listen. You are not looking for their opinion or a solution.
- Alternatively, write down what happened, how you felt, what you could have done to improve the situation or what you shouldn't have done to make matters worse.
- After you have written it down, burn it, learn from it and then let it go for good.
- Alternative therapies such as hypnotherapy can also help trigger past memories and experiences in order for them to be dealt with in the now.
- If you feel your past issues are complicated and not easily expressed, perhaps a qualified counsellor or psychologist can help.

ANOTHER GOOD STRATEGY – EMPTY CHAIR EXERCISE

A great way to deal with past regret is to share your feelings through a simple 'empty chair' exercise. Regrets can include being sorry for past actions, expressing feelings to someone who has hurt you and saying goodbye to someone that you never got the chance to. This exercise is a role play.

- Sit in a chair and place an empty chair in front of you. You imagine the person you wish to speak to is now sitting in the chair in front of you.

- It's time to talk to them, let out the feelings that have been pent up over the years, share the words that you've wanted to say for so long.
- Let out the anger, the tears or frustration, apologise — whatever it is that you need to say to let go, and keep going until you have nothing left.
- After you've done this, I want you to now sit in that same chair in front of you.
- Become the person you had placed in the chair. Put yourself in their shoes.
- Give yourself the response you were hoping for all those years ago. The empathy, the apology, the forgiveness, the words "I love you" — and really mean what you say. This way you get to see two sides of the story, it may shed light on the situation and you may see how it felt to be them.

This role playing exercise is very effective and used by many relationship counsellors. I know it will help you heal and to move forward with your life.

Now you can detach yourself away from that particular time in your life. Let go of those personal wounds, these control dramas that keep you frozen in time. Ask yourself, "What did I learn from this?" There are lessons in everything as we go through this journey called life. If you're willing to open yourself up and listen, your heart will speak to you. By doing this it will be very cathartic and you will see the light of knowing and understand why certain events happen to us in our life.

DON'T OPEN OLD WOUNDS

It's no good for you to keep opening up old wounds all the time, otherwise you will never have a chance to let the wound heal and recover, just like a scab on your skin. The more you pick at it, the longer it will take to heal.

Have you played the game, let's share wounds? This is where you share your personal history with someone and then they have their turn and you compete to see who has had the worst thing happen to them in their life. This is destructive behaviour. Don't play this game as nobody wins. It just makes you feel depressed, your self-esteem drops to an all time low and before you know it, you're looking to escape those moments in your life, and your new reality with an induced perception of reality. An addiction in other words, to take you away from the wounds you have opened up and find a gateway of stress relief. They are usually in the form of alcohol, drugs, gambling, tobacco, high risk sexual activity, over-eating and cruelty. Don't turn to destructive behaviour as a means to escape your unhappy state. It is the exact opposite direction of where you want to be heading in your life.

When you create these energy blocks which suppress your true self through addiction, your emotional and mental imbalances will remain. Until you reach your pain threshold and say, "I can't do this anymore!" and commit and persevere with clearing these blockages, you will come to an awareness of why you are acting out in this particular way and this will be the first glimpse of a new you.

> Beware of dissipating your powers; strive
> constantly to concentrate them.
> – JOHANN WOLFGANG VON GOETHE

STOP FEELING GUILTY – TAKE CHARGE OF YOUR LIFE

It's time to stop feeling guilty for what has happened to you in the past or what you may have done in the past. You have a responsibility to yourself to let go of this self-destructive behaviour and stop avoiding what you need to do now.

Take charge of your life, bring yourself back into the moment and reclaim what is rightly yours — you. Stop disempowering yourself and needing the approval of others. This is self-defeating and won't do you any good. It's time to approve of yourself again, you're worthy. Accept yourself for who you are, don't play the manipulation game. It's growth, change and awareness that you're looking for, not disappointment and disillusionment.

> Nothing so needs reforming as other people's habits.
> – MARK TWAIN

STRATEGIES FOR FAVOURABLE OUTCOMES

If you want to empower yourself in the now, look into the past at those experiences where you achieved favourable results. I've outlined some examples below to get you started, so you can come up with your own.

- When you did well on your last exam, identify the process leading up to the exam. You may have studied at a particular time of the day, on your own or with a tutor. Using this experience, perhaps there are study methods which work that you can apply into other areas of your life.
- Remember the last time you did an excellent presentation in front of work colleagues. How did you prepare for it? Did you clear your mind so you stayed focused? Did you meditate before hand? Whatever strategy you used, the same might also work for you when you are next in a stressful situation.
- Perhaps you gave an eloquent speech in front of a large crowd. You may have rehearsed so many times a day for a week to ensure you were prepared. Preparation can be incorporated in many areas of your life.
- On the sport field or golf course when you played particularly well, think back to that experience. Perhaps you had the encouragement from another team member or player, which spurred you on to achieve victory. In other areas of your life, having supportive and encouraging people around you can help you achieve favourable results.

As you can see, you can learn valuable lessons from past experiences. You can also identify those experiences that you don't want to repeat, or from other people's experiences, whether they be good or bad, it's all valuable for our learning. We become what we know and we learn by what we see. Let the past be your mentor, it will help guide you.

Reminiscing can be a very powerful tool in achieving what you desire. Embracing those thoughts and feelings you once felt in the past will help you overcome any challenge or obstacle in the present moment.

As soon as you come to this conclusion, to keep your energy and focus for yourself right now, the more ambition and dedication you'll have to achieve a more positive and favourable outcome.

ENERGY WITHDRAWALS

Okay, imagine this, I use this analogy with my clients and it will give you a good understanding of how we leak our energy and zest for life by looking back into the past and forward into the future, on a daily basis.

Think of your body as an energy automatic teller machine where you go to withdraw your energy and vitality instead of money at the bank. Now, during the course of a day, let's say you're thinking about your last break-up, that's 10%, and then you think about how you were picked on at school as a child, that's 15%. You start to think how tough it was for you, growing up in your childhood home, that's 10%. You're feeling really annoyed about a work colleague that put you on the spot in front of your boss about an hour ago, so that's 20%. So, in total you have made a withdrawal of 55% of your energy for today. I'm getting tired just writing this, but this is how we act. But wait — there's more.

You start thinking about your friends' party on the weekend, what you're going to wear and who will be there, that's 10%. Then there's the overseas holiday you've got planned in five months, you can't wait to get there and eat the beautiful food, and enjoy the glorious scenery, that's 10%. You have a thought that there is nothing in the fridge for dinner tonight, so you start working out a plan of what you want and when can you get to the shops, that's another 5%. So, there goes an additional 25% for our energy and vitality for the day.

So when we add up our past energy withdrawals 55% and future withdrawals 25%, in total 80% is leaking our vitality. It's no wonder we can't muster up any motivation or willpower to achieve what we want for today and live the life of our dreams.

Your body is in a state of emotional and mental bankruptcy. Let go of inner emptiness and fill your soul full of vitality and zest for yourself by only concentrating on today.

> I never think of the future, it comes soon enough.
> – ALBERT EINSTEIN

LET GO OF DESTRUCTIVE BEHAVIOUR

Imagine a bucket full of water placed in front of you at height level. Each time you think of the past or the future, I want you to puncture a hole in the bucket. You will see the water draining from the bucket, that's your energy, being drained each time you talk about the past, opening up old wounds, being a passive bystander in your life, being controlled or manipulated by the past, the events and experiences.

Let go of this destructive behaviour for good. It's time to let go of self-pity, playing the martyr, or being dominated by past events. Are you ready to participate in your own rescue or do you want to stay right here and wallow in your misery? I know misery loves company but it's time to become the few and not the many. What do you say? Are you ready? Raise your attitude to new heights, become more positive and say goodbye to the old you.

If you're living like this, your mind will be full of noise and your thoughts will be very scattered and confused throughout the day. How can you remain focused on the present if you don't have enough energy and zest for this moment?

Don't you think it's time you reclaimed your energy from the past and out of the future and, kept all your energy for today?

> To different minds, the same world is a hell, and a heaven.
> — RALPH WALDO EMERSON

BUILDING YOUR ENERGY BALANCE

To start making deposits back into your life and giving yourself zest and vitality for living in the now, you have to get back to basics. Below are some simple strategies you can undertake to build your energy balance.

- Surround yourself with interesting and beautiful people that inspire and motivate you.
- Start enjoying what you love to do and make time to do it.
- Start a hobby or artistic pursuit. Take up photography, get into the garden, start a journal or paint.
- Get into a healthy way of living, eat properly, exercise daily, take the dog for a walk.
- Become more positive in your attitude towards yourself and life in general.
- Start meditating to quiet your mind and listen to your heart. Meditation will be covered in further detail in chapter 10.
- Ask yourself, "What have I been thinking about for months, but haven't taken the initiative to begin?" Maybe it's the new course in floristry or learning Italian.
- The more active and interested you become in yourself and your life, and begin to enjoy the now, the sooner your life will become a place where dreams do come true.

This is how you reclaim back love for yourself and life. By being involved with the things you love to do, you're drawing back energy that you've lost or given away. Soon you'll be enthusiastic and have the desire to do more in the present moment. All we have is this moment. Love it, embrace it.

If you have children or if you know someone who has children, I suggest you take the time and observe them carefully. Watch how they get caught up in the moment. We have a lot to learn from and admire about these beautiful little people. Look at how focused they are playing with their friends or with their toys. Totally absorbed in the moment, now that's what I mean by living in the now.

BE MINDFUL

As of tomorrow, I would like you to totally absorb yourself into what you're doing every moment of the day. Try it and see how you go. For example, when having your breakfast in the morning, take the time to enjoy the ritual of preparing your breakfast.

Take your ingredients out of the cupboard or fridge, prepare the meal, and sit down in front of it. Look at what you're eating, smell it, admire it, take the time to chew your food more slowly. Enjoy the taste and nourishment you get from this food. The sensations you may get will be multiplied as you are ever present in the now and you're totally focused on what you're doing, eating and enjoying your first meal of the day.

Savour it without any interruptions or thoughts about what happened to you yesterday or last week or what you have to do today. This is called mindful eating.

Now, I would like you to carry on this same ritual throughout the day. While at work, concentrate on doing only one task at a time. This includes checking your emails, or eating your lunch. With this new sense of peace and freedom, you'll find you have more energy to complete your tasks to a higher than standard outcome. Your mind will be peaceful and more focused and there will be a strong sense of accomplishment. This will give you confidence throughout the day, making you operate at a slower pace but with greater results and a greater sense of achievement. This is called mindful living. Give it a try, what have you got to lose?

If you find that your mind starts to wonder, I want you to ask yourself these questions:
1. Where am I? Answer — **HERE**
2. What time is it? Answer — **NOW**

Asking yourself these two simple questions will help your mind from becoming racy, help you refocus and put you back in the now.

> Reality is created by the mind.
> – PLATO

BE IN THE NOW

When you get into the routine of living your life like this, the past and the future will no longer exist to you. What will exist is the beautiful, euphoric feeling of flow and where time goes by really fast because you're so wrapped up in the moment. This is where happiness and joy can be found, not yesterday or tomorrow.

ENJOY YOUR JOURNEY

From this very moment, start to enjoy your journey and not the destination. When looking for a better tomorrow, we're always looking at the end result and think to ourselves, "When this happens, I'll be happy". But what is actually happening is you're putting your happiness on hold. You're not realising it's the doing that makes you grow and change, parts of your character that you didn't even know you had in you, develop and change you from inside out. Your happiness comes from inside yourself, not the other way around. Understand you become a better person now not tomorrow, as tomorrow may never come. All we have is this moment.

I used to live my life like this. "When I finish school, I'll be happy and have freedom. When I get a job, I'll move out of my parents' house, have my own place and I'll be happy. When I start my new job, I'm sure my boss will be better than the last one, and I can't wait to go on my overseas trip in the next six months where I'll be free from my boring job and life".

This is no way to live a happy life. As you can see there is a recurring theme here. I'm always waiting for something good to happen so I can be happy but instead I should be enjoying the now, and the journey, this is where real happiness and freedom exists.

If you are living your life like this or if this sounds familiar to you, I want you to draw the strength and courage to understand that your life is what is happening to you right now and what you're doing with it, counts right now. Not six months ago or six weeks from now.

YOU NEVER KNOW

I would like to share a great folk tale about living in the now and what a positive mindset can do for you when life delivers challenges. By being in the now and having a positive attitude, you can handle anything that comes your way.

> There was a farmer who owned a beautiful stallion which ran away. The farmer relied on the horse as his only means of transport. His neighbour commented what a terrible thing that was to happen, and the farmer simply replied, "You never know".
>
> A week goes by and his stallion returns with more horses following to fill the farmer's stables. His neighbour comments about how lucky the farmer is. The farmer responds, "You never know."
>
> A month later the farmer's son is riding one of the wild horses that came back with the stallion and he fell off and broke his leg. The neighbour said, "That's a tragedy your son is the only worker on your farm." The farmer responded, "You never know".
>
> Soon following, the government came through the village conscripting young men for service to fight the war, however because the young man's leg was broken he couldn't be conscripted and was left behind. The neighbour said, "That's great, what a blessing in disguise, your son doesn't have to go and fight in a war." The farmer said, "You never know!"

This is one of my favourite stories. Next time life throws adversity at you, be calm, relax and be in the moment because you know why? You just never know! Sometimes hardship can be a blessing in disguise.

> Sometimes we turn to God when our foundations are shaking, only to find out that it is God that is shaking them.
> – ANONYMOUS

I don't want you to miss any more opportunities for today. Don't put off living for the now. I want you to jump off this beginnings and endings treadmill. Take a huge bite of life and enjoy and savour the now.

Remember the past and the future is your mind playing games with you, they are illusions, make no mistake about that. It's time to become the best version of yourself, are you ready? Stay focused, enjoy the journey and always be forever present in the amazing gift called life …Now!!!!!

> You are a child of the universe, no less than the stars and trees, and you have a right to be here. And whether or not it is clear to you, no doubt the universe is unfolding as it should be.
> – DESIDERATA

FIVE

What are you up to?

> Life belongs to the living and he who lives must be prepared for changes.
> — JOHANN WOLFGANG VON GOETHE

Now that I've got you living in the moment and you have an understanding of how important this moment really is, I would like to ask you, "What are you doing with it?" Are you in a job which you find satisfying and rewarding? Do you enjoy and are you happy with the relationship that you're in? Are you miserable and like to complain about your dead end job or your loveless relationship? It's easier just to do nothing about your unhappiness.

To really enjoy life and all of its beautiful moments and great experiences, you need to ask questions about how happy you are in life and your place in it. You're so worthy of living the life that you want to, but you have to make the choice — do you want to settle for mediocrity, or wake up each day excited about being you and all the wonders that life can offer you and you can offer it.

JOBS, PARTNERS AND UNCONDITIONAL LOVE

Think about this for a moment, is the job you turn up to every day giving you the stimulation and excitement that you want out of a career? Let's face it, if you're going to work for the next fifty years, you might as well get job satisfaction, be happy turning up every day and being appreciated for your effort, time and hard work? Or maybe sometimes you feel that you're just a number and you're going through the motions of another day and if you left tomorrow, your job would be filled by someone else. Perhaps you feel that life would just go on, regardless if you're at work or not?

What about your relationships with your partner, friends and family? Are they giving you the love and respect you deserve and that your heart yearns for as a human being? When was the last time you told your loved ones that you loved them and thanked them for being a part of your life and that you cherish the times you have together?

Do it now while they're still alive, if there's someone close to you now tell them, watch their reaction and watch how good you make them feel and how it makes you feel.

Love is what we're here on earth to learn, to love unconditionally. Tell your loved ones how you feel. Live in the moment, because all moments are very sacred to us, one life one chance.

CLOSE CONNECTIONS

When we develop close connections with people not only does it make us feel great, but everybody deserves to know they're loved, valued and appreciated. It also boosts their self-worth and confidence as well as our own, and puts a big smile on their face.

When we feel love and respect for ourselves, we can take that sense of inner confidence and self-worth to the job market and look for work that makes us happy, where our time is valued and appreciated and where making a contribution to society makes a difference and where everyone benefits, not just us. It is in the giving that we receive.

WORK LIFE BALANCE

Have you ever thought about the amount of hours you put into your job and give to employers compared to time spent with loved ones? Do you realise you spend more time with your work colleagues than your partner and family? It's actually very sad and a lot of the working population are in the same boat. Work life balance is needed here.

But all of this is about to change. Do you want to work fewer hours, make more money, have job satisfaction, and be fulfilled by the work that you do? Would you like to spend more time with your loved ones, take fantastic holidays and be able to afford life's little pleasures without having to put it on the credit card and sell your soul for it?

Okay, so I have your attention? Sounds like I'm selling dreams but I'm not, I'm deadly serious and all of this is up for the taking. You can live the life you want, make the money you want, land your dream job and have meaningful relationships with family and friends and live a life worth living, but it's all up to you! It's your choice.

But, to get there and enjoy your new way of living, I want you to answer this simple question, but it's a question that will change your life. Answer truthfully otherwise you will miss the opportunity to achieve everything in life that is close to your heart. How much sowing, effort and action are you putting into your life to achieve the rewards that you so rightly deserve and seek?

YOU REAP WHAT YOU SOW

What are you doing today to better your tomorrow? Where do you think you'll be in two years time? You will arrive, but the question is where? If you haven't worked on yourself in the last two years, you'll be in the same place in the next two years! Until you decide to change.

Understand your life is like a garden. You must take care and watch out for the weeds (problems), before they take over. Take the time to nourish the soil (positive thoughts and beliefs) and turn it over. Cultivate (action and effort) and plant seeds (positive habits and behaviours) so you can create a successful beautiful garden (life). Are you taking care of your garden?

> Each man reaps on his own farm.
> – PLAUTUS

Now look at your life and understand that everything you have in your life, your beliefs, your attitudes, your job, your relationship all of your material possessions is a result of what you have put into your life up until this very moment.

There is a universal law called cause and effect, or to me, I call it you reap what you sow and for every action you do, you either get back an equal or opposite reaction. Our whole lives are based on this law today and until we die. What you do to others you'll get back in return and this one law works for every facet in our education called life.

When you get serious about changing your life and start working on yourself, life is going to get a lot easier on you. It's just the same with this law, you must be ready to put the hard work in now and life will start working for you, not against you. Build your life, like you build a house with strong foundations. You must be prepared to work on yourself. Turn ideas into reality. Let activity produce new beginnings.

Treat yourself with respect and people will start respecting you as well. Work smarter at your job, do your job better than anybody else in your workplace and become amazed at the results. You'll become noticed because you stand out above the rest. Start giving more of yourself into your relationships and watch the subtle changes in family, friends and strangers and watch them return the favour in kind. But the opposite can happen too, judge and criticise people and guess what, it will be given back to you. Treat people with no respect, or rudely and watch them treat you the same.

> Human improvement is from within, outward.
> – JAMES ANTHONY FROUDE

YOUR LIFE IS LIKE A MIRROR

Your life is like a mirror, what you see is what you get. In your life you may have noticed that what you have been giving out is what has been coming back to you. The way you treat and see people is a reflection of how you want to be treated. If you want friends and you go out looking for them you'll find them scarce, be a friend to yourself and everyone and soon you'll have lots of friends, more than you can handle.

Ask yourself, "Is my life working for me the way that I want it to?" If the answer to this question is "no", it's time to start planting some seeds (action and effort) now. There's a saying, "If you don't like the direction in which you're headed, change directions before you end up where you're headed".

How's life ever going to change if you don't? Do you think everybody around you will change for you to make your life easier? No, not at all!

> Nothing endures but change.
> – HERACLITUS

LIVE A NEW REALITY

It's time for you to live a new reality, change your routine and start taking some risks in your life. To really live and not just exist, you need to get out there and raise the bar on yourself, find your limitations, there are none, only the ones you place upon yourself. Get to know who you really are and live your life to its full potential.

If you don't change, expect much of the same. And, if you're not taking some risks and being adventurous and making changes you'll never have any great moments to look back on, or stories to recall and share.

GET OUT OF YOUR COMFORT ZONE

By playing it safe and keeping yourself in your comfort zone how far has that taken you? Don't you think it's time you took the bull by the horns and said, "Let's do this? I'm ready, willing and able. I've got nothing to lose". Don't you think you owe it to yourself, your family and friends to be happy, enjoy your life and all that it has to offer before it's too late? Well, I do! I think you owe it to yourself to be the best you can be.

There's no such thing as security in this life. We can depart from this mortal coil at any time. Your clothes wear out, your health can deteriorate, your relationships may fail, the money dries up, the workplace can be restructured and you can be made redundant at any moment. The only moment you'll ever find security in your life is when you're improving it.

LIVING IS FOR THE NOW

There's your safety and security for you. If you want safety and security and a life with no problems or worries, go and take a look in the local cemetery, there's a lot of that type of action going on in there. Be my guest. But living is for the now, the moment for freedom, happiness, good times, enjoying what life has to offer, giving back to society and the world on a larger scale. Immerse yourself in life, your life is a blessing and each day you have an opportunity to discover and awaken your giant within.

Think back to when you felt bullet proof, a time when you thought that you were bigger than life. When you took plenty of risks, you were living in the moment and believed you could do anything.

As a nineteen year old I can remember walking into a bakery and seeing the prettiest girl I had ever seen. I asked her for her phone number and she gladly gave it to me. That was a risk that I took and it paid off, I walked out of there ten feet tall!

I can also remember walking out of a mundane boring job, where I worked a lot of hours, I wasn't appreciated or valued, I was getting paid a pittance for my time and finally found the courage to resign. Oh, by the way, does anybody know what this feels like? A couple of weeks later I had a better job, I was much happier getting paid my real worth, had a great boss and enjoyed each day I was there.

How much are you willing to sacrifice to hold onto your job or your relationships? Are they worth your health, your happiness, your freedom to discover what else is out there which could truly make you happy beyond your wildest dreams? Life's about taking chances and taking risks. When was the last time you took one? Be honest!

CHANGE YOUR LIFE

If you're unhappy about your life, change it. If you're unhappy about the way you look or feel, change it. If you're unhappy about your job or relationships, change it. What have you got to lose? Your happiness? You don't even have that! You get the picture, that's great, now change it!

Risk now, take some chances now, tell that person you love them, start your business now, buy that house now, take that overseas holiday to your dream destination now, let go of all your fears, worries and doubts, they're holding you back. If not now, when? Tomorrow is too late. You can start with small steps initially and plant the seeds for a better future. Start studying, go back to college to gain a qualification, begin that course to learn something new to improve your mind and job prospects. We should never stop learning and there are many resources, books and mentors to help.

When you have done this and you're confident within yourself, go out into society and play your role in it. That is real inner fulfilment and happiness.

TAKE CALCULATED RISKS

I'm not telling you to make rash or impulsive decisions, but to take healthy calculated risks and chances. They are healthy for your growth and change in your life. If you don't take a chance and some risks, your life is destined for much of the same. Can you really live with that?

When I look back at my past and take note of all the challenges and obstacles that were put in front of me, I believe this is what has made me the person I am today.

I have made 'mistakes' along the way — I use that word very loosely. Because that word tends to have negative connotations and makes people feel bad, or can make them feel like they're not good enough. So what they do is they stop trying, they give up hope as they don't want to be seen as a failure, so they fall back into old ways so they're not criticised or judged or deemed as a failure.

Just as I pushed through the 'mistakes' you can too. I encourage you for attempting to give it a go and for believing in yourself. The more times you try and do this in life, the better chances you will have of succeeding. Just ask anyone who is leading a happy and fulfilled life.

Commit yourself to learning from your mistakes rather than getting down and upset or you're destined to make the same mistake again. See your mistakes as a learning curve, don't become emotionally attached otherwise you won't see the true value in lessons learnt.

> I make more mistakes than anyone else I know,
> and sooner or later, I patent most of them.
> – THOMAS EDISON

DON'T GIVE UP

Look at the lives of all the people that you admire and have taken our society to the forefront of greatness throughout the centuries. Do you think Einstein, Ford, Emerson, Gates and Branson, just to name a few, gave up after their first hurdle? Of course they didn't, they made plenty of mistakes along the way, the more the better because they are learning experiences. They know how to succeed, they had to hold strong, persevere, and pick themselves up after falling, staying true to their vision and believing in themselves, no matter what other people said. They had courage to dare and push limits and boundaries where others didn't dare, and look where it got them.

You are just like them, you come from the same source, and you can achieve anything you want. There are people around the world right now, doing, making mistakes, dusting themselves off, persevering and putting themselves out there, changing not only their lives but others'. What about you?

> One doesn't discover new lands without consenting to lose sight, for a very long time, of the shore.
> – ANDRE GIDE

START NOW

The sooner you begin and get comfortable taking chances and risks the easier life will start opening up pathways and doors to your new reality. Areas which have lain dormant in your life for such a long time will now sprout new opportunities for you to discover and enjoy, it's yours for the taking. Open that door or climb out of the window, I don't care, take the initiative and then prospects become limitless.

> Whatever you can do or dream you can do, begin it.
> Boldness has genius, magic and power in it.
> Begin it now.
> – JOHANN WOLFGANG VON GOETHE

When you look at your new lease on life, you won't look back at your failures as they are only stepping stones towards greatness.

It's your time to choose to live this life and go beyond, take some chances and risks. Start sowing some seeds now (action and effort) for a greater, more fruitful harvest. Are you the master gardener of your life? Or are you going to stick with what you know and isn't working for you? Are you going to stay inside your little bubble, holding onto your security blanket and watching your life pass you by another day, week, month and year? Start climbing your way to the very top. You can do it!

> He who rejects change is the architect of decay. The only human institution which rejects progress is the cemetery.
> – HAROLD WILSON

SIX
Enough with the excuses

> He that is good for making excuses is seldom good for anything else.
> – BENJAMIN FRANKLIN

Now, what I would like you to do is draw your attention to all the people you admire in your life. Those that are in their dream job, who travel every year, having meaningful relationships, are always cheery, and are a pleasure to be around when in their company.

Turn your focus to the people who are the exact opposite of these people. You know the ones that have a sad face, are unhappy and miserable and generally complaining about their health or something that's an inconvenience for them. Most of the time after speaking to them, you feel drained physically or if you see them in public and they don't see you, you run the other way. We all know someone like this and we all have done this, at some time in our lives because we didn't have enough energy to listen to them whine.

Have you ever stopped and wondered what makes these two groups of people so different in the way they go about living their lives? One group lives such a happy and interesting life, while the other group finds life a chore and struggle just to get through every day. For them each day brings the same as the last, with only fleeting moments of happiness but no true fulfilment to speak about.

There's only one ingredient to the winning formula which makes the positive, happy and successful people achieve and lead such exciting and interesting lives compared to the other unhappy, unfulfilled group. Have you worked it out yet? Do you know what the difference is? Ok, I'll tell you!

> To change one's life, start immediately, do it
> flamboyantly, no exceptions, no excuses.
> – WILLIAM JAMES

YOUR LIFE, YOUR CHOICE

The people who are living the life that they want to are the ones that have made a **choice** to live this way. They know through action and effort and having a plan of action (there's that secret formula again) or should I say, winning formula — they increase the odds of achieving their desirable outcomes to live happy and sustainable lives. They also realise the more times they put themselves into the position of obtaining their goals and raising the bar on themselves more often than not, they will succeed. These people see failure only as stepping stones to greatness and they never give up on themselves. They have come to understand life is too short and they would rather live life on their feet, than die on their knees.

Then we have the unhappy group who are despondent, their lives go around in circles and they will tell everybody about their misfortunes and how badly they have been mistreated throughout their lives. They never really achieve their dreams or succeed, as they only see dreams coming true in the movies and they believe dreams are out of their grasp.

There is only one thing though that this group does have over the other group and they have a lot of it in abundance, more than the successful, happier group. Do you know what it is?

EXCUSES

Excuses, they can be endless. Whether they're bad excuses or good excuses, they both weigh the same and do exactly the same thing. They stop you from living the life that you want. They make people sit on the sidelines of life, feeling left out, miserable, not being able to get into the thrill and the chase of life.

When you're on the sidelines of life, you're putting your contribution for yourself and the wider community on hold. You can't display or use your natural born talents and abilities for the greater good. That's the tragedy of it all, wasted talent and the feeling of belonging to a greater purpose, in which you're not obtaining or fulfilling. All excuses are negative beliefs that limit people's potential in the now.

Ok, now you can see the difference between the two groups and the consequences they both receive due to their actions, or a lack thereof. The happier, more successful group who enjoy waking up each morning, don't have time for reasons why they can't enjoy life and get on with what they have to do. By making time each day, they put in the required effort to achieve the positive results to get them where they want to go. They are willing to do whatever it takes to see their dreams turn into a reality. The unhappier group, who get what life gives them (which isn't much), will give excuse after excuse of why they can't enjoy their lives.

Usually their excuses play to the tune of something like this. I was brought up into the wrong family and nobody loves me. I didn't get enough schooling or I didn't finish school, so I'm not educated enough. I don't have enough money to go through college, my kids need me and the government make it so hard to live these days.

> Each player must accept the cards life deals him or her. But once they are in hand, he or she must decide how to play the cards in order to win the game.
> – VOLTAIRE

BLAME GAME

When it comes down to it, for most people who dish out excuses and reasons why they can't do it, usually it's an inconvenience to them and they would rather play the blame game than to put in the required effort and hard work to achieve what is necessary to get the most out of their lives. Happy, successful people concentrate on solutions, while those who blame, focus on problems. Unfortunately, the only thing they get out of this destructive routine of living is that their excuses are used up and the only real reason was they didn't even try.

Remember our lives are gifts given to us, not our given right. Don't become complacent. You owe it to yourself to be the best version of yourself and to the wider community in general.

FEAR OF FAILURE

I'm sure at one time or another you may have blamed or given these excuses to stop you from living your dreams. We do this for many reasons, mainly a fear of failure, fear of not being good enough, fear of rejection or what other people may say about us, so we don't do anything at all. So, what we do is get back in our boxes; we fall into line; like little sheep we follow the herd and become 'sheeple'. Never let the voices of others drown out your own inner voice.

> I have often wondered how it should come to pass, that every man loving himself best, should more regard other men's opinions concerning himself than his own. For if any God or grave master standing by, should command any of us to think nothing by himself but what he should presently speak out; no man were able to endure it, though but for one day. Thus do we fear more what our neighbours will think of us, than what we ourselves.
> — MARCUS AURELIUS

TALL POPPIES DON'T MAKE EXCUSES

An old Japanese proverb says, "The nail that stands out above the rest is always the first to get hit." Unfortunately, this happens in our society and has been going on since the dawn of time. It's also known as tall poppy syndrome, a social trend in which successful and distinguished people are criticised or resented because their achievements make them stand out from the crowd, or what is considered 'normal'.

These people are successful and notable in their fields because they test the limits and boundaries of life's restraints. They are usually targeted for their challenging and unconventional thinking. Excuses don't exist for these people as they are totally free and embrace their individuality, uniqueness and also applaud others when they do the same. Do you know someone like this? Are they a thrill to be around or are they a bore and draining to your life's energy? As George Herbert says, "Storms make the oak grow deeper roots". Let go of all of this, set your own mark in this life. Stand out from the crowd, dare to be different, dare to dream. It's usually the bystanders in life that haven't achieved their goals and dreams that try and knock others down. This is your life; it's yours for the choosing, dream big, aim high.

> Great spirits have always encountered violent opposition from mediocre minds.
> — ALBERT EINSTEIN

BELIEVE IN YOURSELF

People right now from all walks of life are overcoming numerous odds to achieve the impossible. Stay strong, have the discipline, be persistent and most of all be unshakeable. Be a giant walking amongst ants. Believe in yourself, because I do!

> People are always blaming their circumstances for what they are. I don't believe in circumstances. The people who get on in this world are the people who get up and look for the circumstances they want, and if they can't find them, they make them.
> — *GEORGE BERNARD SHAW*

SEVEN

Change your thoughts, change your life

> The mind is the master over every kind of fortune, it acts in both ways, being the cause of its own happiness and its own misery.
> — SENECA

For me to the write this book for you is a dream come true. When you believe in yourself and act accordingly the world is your oyster and it's yours for the taking. Everything can be yours as long as you have the courage, the drive, motivation and a strong faith in your abilities and talents. You will be rewarded with a successful consciousness and outcome, in all given hours.

Your thoughts create your reality. When you have such belief in yourself and you realise that positive thoughts can create such powerful forces in the way you create your reality, the impossible becomes possible. There are those in this life think they can and will, and those who think they can't and won't.

> Let a prince be guarded with soldiers, attended by counsellors, and protected by a fort, yet if his thoughts disturb him, he is miserable.
> — PLUTARCH

LIKE ATTRACTS ALIKE

Positivity will attract positivity and negativity will attract negativity. Your thoughts are energy. Can you remember at the beginning of this book when I was talking about energy and vibration and how everything in our physical reality is a vibrant energy system?

Your subconscious mind sends out signals, just like your radio or television although you can't see them, you know they're out there in the energy matrix waiting to be received and acted upon. This is a very powerful frequency and it also works the exact opposite as well, which is being negative. The more positive you are, the higher the frequency of your signal and the more dominant it will be over the negative thoughts and lower frequencies.

LAW OF NATURAL VIBRATION

The law of natural vibration governs, controls and destroys any lower rate of vibration. Positive action, thought visualisation and beliefs will always reign supreme over any negative thoughts and actions applied, because being positive holds a higher, more dominating force.

> Thought takes a man out of servitude into freedom.
> — RALPH WALDO EMERSON

AFFIRMATIONS

Another way of achieving a positive mindset and outlook in your life is to use affirmations which vibrate your intentions and send out strong signals to the energy web (universe) around us. Remember at the beginning of the book, I explained how positive words resonate at a higher frequency than negative words and how they boost your immune system and how you feel physically and psychologically? When strong positive words are said as a statement such as, "I feel great, life is wonderful", "It's possible", "I can handle it", these will put you in a positive frame of mind and you can enjoy your day.

Understand it's our words that direct our thoughts and emotions and it's a choice you make about how you think and the language which you use to express yourself. Words are very powerful and the intentions behind them can either lift you to great heights or make you feel miserable and depressed.

Let's say you have to make a presentation at work, you could repeat to yourself, "A great presentation," and believing it makes it so, let go of any details because you will block the message and frequency of your statement. If you are ill and you want to get better you can say, "Every day and in every way I'm getting better and better". This statement will resonate with you to boost your immune system and give it the energy that it needs for recovery. If you don't want to say this aloud say it in your mind, write it down on a note.

I have small sticky notes scattered around my home including on the fridge and on the bedside table so I can see my affirmations when I am going about my everyday living, including when I first wake up in the morning. You could place your affirmations as a screen saver on your computer, whatever works for you, just make sure it's a place you will see often. This is just another mind power technique to help you change your thoughts and your life.

DEVELOP YOUR CONSCIOUSNESS

Now, what I have just described to you can be done in every aspect of your life. If you want to play better golf, develop a golf consciousness. Believe, think, act like you are a better player and in time with repetition and visualisation and practice, the subconscious mind will make it so. If you want better health, get more health consciousness, better relationships with loved ones, and get great relationship consciousness. You get the idea, begin now, don't give up and most importantly fake it till you make it.

There is much truth to this as the subconscious mind doesn't know the difference between reality and non-reality. But it will take on the most governing force, whether it is positive or negative, it's your choice.

POSITIVE VISUALISATION

There have been many experiments over the years in regards to positive visualisation. Positive visualisation is the forming of positive images in your mind to program your subconscious.

Many years ago a research experiment was undertaken using three groups of basketball players to test their ability at scoring hoops. The first group undertook physical training and practised shooting hoops every day for a month. The second group didn't shoot hoops at all and the third group visualised themselves for half an hour each day shooting and scoring hoops in their minds, virtually.

Here are the results — the first group who practiced physically improved by 24 percent. The second group showed no improvement. The third group, who visualised themselves making the shots and scoring, improved just as much as the group that practised physically.

This demonstrates how powerful positive visualisation really is and when it's directed in the right way, you can bring about positive change in all aspects of your life — sport, health, work, relationships and special events in your life where you want successful outcomes. By directing your positive thoughts and visualisations out into the energy web and being confident about demanding a positive outcome for yourself, you will soon realise there are no limits to what you can achieve apart from the illusionary ones you place upon yourself.

Thoughts are so powerful that it's a well-known fact that some of the people who visit their local general practitioner suffer from psychosomatic illness. People talk themselves into getting some type of illness and the body acts accordingly. For example, have you or somebody you know said, "Winter is coming, I'm always good for a cold or two," and sure enough without fail, they get a cold. Then you have another person who says they never get sick and sure enough they never get sick, even when everyone around them is sick in bed with the flu.

What's happening here is that people are unknowingly bringing up the past programs of what happened to them last winter and the subconscious mind will bring to them what they are thinking. So, please take note, all health care professionals, it's wise to use the appropriate words as they can either help or hinder your patient's recovery.

> The mind is a great healer.
> – HIPPOCRATES

THE BODY'S REACTION TO NEGATIVITY

Another reason not to think negatively and not hold on to fear, anger, hate, frustration, resentment and past negative memories is because when we feel these emotions they impact our nervous system. The body releases cortisol, which is a hormone that makes the body feel sick and low in vibration, in turn lowering the frequency, which makes you feel heavy and lethargic.

Every time you think negative or bring up negative feelings the subconscious mind doesn't know the difference between reality and non reality. It goes by what it knows to be true and what you have programmed it to believe.

When cortisol is released into the blood stream, the body becomes acidic, lowering the immune system and this is how people become sick and depressed. All because of their negative thoughts and feelings! It makes you think twice about being negative doesn't it? You have a choice of how you feel and your reactions to your challenges. It's time to take control of what happens to you in every moment of your day. Step back for a moment, take a few big deep breaths and take charge of your thoughts, mentally and emotionally. The way that you handle yourself will be a lot more positive.

> The greatest revolution in our generation is the discovery that human beings, by changing the inner attitudes of their minds can change the outer aspects of their lives. It is too bad that most people will not accept this tremendous discovery and begin living it.
> – WILLIAM JAMES

THE TWO WOLVES

This is a story of an old Cherokee chief, who is sharing a story with his grandson about a battle that goes on in each one of us.

> The old and wise chief tells his grandson that within each of us are two wolves — one dark and one light. One is evil, full of anger, rage, jealousy, sorrow, self-pity, lies, inferiority and doubt. The other wolf is filled with love, joy, compassion, hope, peace, empathy and truth. The grandson asks his grandfather, "Which wolf wins?" The wise old warrior replies, "The one you feed."

This story is so true! What wolf are you feeding? Take a look around you and reflect now on your life and your environment. It's a reflection on your thoughts and behaviour and how you're directing it. Is it time to feed the other wolf?

The best remedy for life is to have strong positive thoughts always going through your conscious mind. We have over 50,000 single thoughts a day. That's a lot isn't it? Remember 90 percent of our thoughts are from our subconscious mind.

THE GLASS IS HALF FULL

There are two groups of people in life, those who perceive the glass is half empty or half full, which one are you? Our thoughts can work for us and help us or work against us and hinder our development and growth and let decay settle in. What we focus on, we become.

OUR MINDS ARE POWERFUL TOOLS

As human beings our minds are the most powerful tools we have been given to shape and alter our lives for the greater good. Because we have free will, we are given a choice.

Our minds are like magnets and the mind will gravitate in the direction of the most influencing thought whether it is positive or negative. I know that positive thought patterns will be beneficial to living the life of your dreams. There will always be sunshine even when it's raining. That's right, being optimistic is a way of life because it will change your life. Believe it, visualise it, live it, think it, do it and it will be so. It's natural law.

> All truly wise thoughts have been thought already a thousand times; but to make them truly ours, we must think them over again honestly, til they take root in our personal experience.
> – JOHANN WOLFGANG VON GOETHE

TRAIN FOR A POSITIVE OUTLOOK

There's always some training to be involved for you to achieve your new positive outlook. As we are all creatures of habit and behaviour, it will take some time to change our patterns of reality but in time, day after day, the results will be amazing.

A VISUALISATION EXERCISE

Imagine now that you have an eye dropper in your hand and it's filled with pink dye. In front of you is a pool full of crystal clear water. Now, this is how change takes place and how the pace of change takes time. Squeeze the eye dropper a drop at a time in the pool. Is the pink dye changing the colour of the pool? Of course it isn't, but with perseverance and action and over time, each day the water in the pool will eventually change colour from crystal clear to pink.

It's the same with our positive thoughts, habits and actions, it takes time to bring about a new way of thinking, just like the colour of the pool. It doesn't happen overnight, but it will happen! Don't give up. If you've been thinking and acting a certain way for a long time, you must have patience and in time you will see a change and so will others see it in you. The rewards are fantastic and endless. I believe if you change your mindset to a positive one you will be so glad you did. Now, start changing your life, a step, or was that a drop, at a time!

To change anything in your life you must first become aware of your thoughts that you are letting enter your mind. You must listen and monitor your thoughts and see how positive or negative they are. Remember this, our thoughts shape the world we live in. You are consciousness; your consciousness creates your reality. Listen and embrace silence, your true spirit wants to shine through you.

> The Universe is change; our life is what our thoughts make it.
> — MARCUS AURELIUS

YOUR OUTER ENVIRONMENT MIRRORS YOUR MENTAL STATE

You can tell a lot about someone by looking at them, their body language and by the way they live their lives. How clean is your home, your office space, your car? You can really get a good indication of what's going on inside someone's mind and their internal thoughts by their external environments.

If your thoughts and mind are negative, messy and confused it's going to be the same in reality as well. There has to be a balance with the way you think and the way you act, both have to be of the same frequency and congruent, otherwise an imbalance occurs and confusion and stagnant energy settles in and takes over your life.

> Each heart is a world. You find all within yourself that you find without. The world that surrounds you is the magic glass of the world within you.
> — JOHANN KASPAR LAVATER

Don't let negativity enter your conscious mind. Confusion, anger, doubt, fear, criticism, and past mistakes and memories of past failures need to be dealt with head on. Believe you're good enough, expect the best for yourself, have faith and trust that your unique talents and abilities will conquer any problem (or should I say a challenge) that comes your way, you will have the mental strength to handle it. Choose positive emotions to motivate and direct you to a positive outcome which creates habits that work for you, not hinder you.

You must take action to become more positive in your life, get energised. Don't just sit around and think positively, it's just not going to fall into your lap. Think, act and visualise. You must let go of the old to make way for the new.

> **Thoughts are things**
> I hold it true that thoughts are things
> They're endowed with bodies and breath and wings
> And that we send them forth to fill
> The world with good results, or ill
> That which we call our secret thought
> Speeds forth to earth's remotest spot

> Leaving its blessings or its woes
> Like tracks behind it as it goes
> We build our future, thought by thought
> For good or ill, yet know it not
> Yet, so the universe was wrought
> Thought is another name for fate
> Choose, then thy destiny and wait
> For love brings love and hate brings hate.
> — HENRY VAN DYKE

SUCCESS BREEDS SUCCESS

Understand, that when you become motivated to do more in your life, you desire to achieve more, you'll get a powerful drive to put the effort in, like a steam train, we build up momentum. Momentum with self-confidence, self-worth then becomes so strong that your faith and trust in your abilities becomes so abundant to yourself and everyone around you, people want to help and be a part of the process. That's why successful people are always surrounded by teams of successful people, and people in general want to be a part of something special, because it makes them feel good. It's a win-win, guaranteed.

It will take practice, just like going to the gym to build biceps or get fit. After one session you won't notice a change, but once you've got the ball rolling momentum is in place, after three months you'll notice an increase in your muscles or fitness. It takes time, perseverance, patience and a positive outlook. To be the best you have to think the best, to expect the best, a bit of hard work never killed anybody. Action is everything. Your health, happiness, relationships and career, everything in your life depends on your positive thoughts and the way you think.

> It seldom happens that a man changes his life through his habitual reasoning. No matter how fully he may sense the new plans and aims revealed to him by reason, he continues to plod along in the old paths until his life becomes frustrating and unbearable...he finally makes the change only when his usual life can no longer be tolerated.
> — LEO TOLSTOY

EIGHT

Let the creativity flow

> Imagination is the beginning of creation.
> You imagine what you desire; you will what you imagine;
> and at last you create what you will.
> — GEORGE BERNARD SHAW

When we feel stagnant in our lives we feel empty like a barren and dried up creek bed, because our actions and efforts aren't getting the required results. Our habits and behaviours are like old worn out socks full of holes, and the pair of them just don't do the same useful job.

We've lost the joy, fun and zest from of our lives and we need to discover a new way of living. All we need is a spark of inspiration to light the excitement back into our lives. Don't you think it's time for you to tap into that right hemisphere of your brain, the more creative, intuitive, colourful and non-linear way to live?

The majority of people live every day by predominately using the left side of their brain. It's more rational, analytical, logical and mathematical. I believe to walk with both feet in my life, I need to use both sides of my brain — one side to keep me grounded (left) and the other to tap into the universal library of infinite intelligence (right) so I can listen and follow my heart (intuition) and create a balance with both sides of my mind.

It's time to dust off the right side of your brain, clear out all the cobwebs and clutter. There's a better, new innovative way to be in this world. You've been there before, some of you still have it, but for those who don't, let me take you back to when you were a child.

THE CREATIVITY OF CHILDHOOD

When we were younger, we had such a strong inherent ability to absorb everything in sight, using all of our senses. The way we learned was to try new things and make mistakes along the way. There was no fear of ridicule from our friends, nobody cared, we had fun and enjoyed ourselves. Our imaginations were our best friends, dreaming, visualising, exploring and discovering these were glorious times. To us, it was normal behaviour. To our parents and older people, we were being creative. As children, our lives each day were a mysterious and surprising gift, like the gifts we received on our birthdays. Can you remember using your imagination and creativity as a child?

> I am enough of the artist to draw freely upon my imagination.
> Imagination is more important than knowledge. Knowledge is limited.
> Imagination encircles the world.
> – ALBERT EINSTEIN

As children we made decisions based on what felt right to us (intuition). We would ask as many questions as possible until we grasped the new concept and our curiosity had been answered. We had the ability to explore our ideas and everybody always gave it a go. We threw our whole hearts into our playing and projects (passion) which took our fancy. Inspiration and enthusiasm could be found in every kindergarten, backyard, park and garage with young children playing. Creativity was pouring out of us and into the environment we surrounded ourselves in. The paintings, the pictures and cubby houses we built, the slippery slide, bow and arrows and peg guns we manufactured, as well as the costumes we made — including cowboys and Indians, sailors and explorers and ghosts — these were great times.

We didn't even know what creativity was let alone know how to pronounce it. We were happy and free-spirited, enjoying each other's company and individuality. Everyone was willing to discover new ways of having more fun and living for each second without hesitation and discovering new possibilities every day and no two days were the same. So what happened?

WHERE IS YOUR CREATIVITY HIDDEN?

Who took the jam out of our donuts? When did most of our creativity run away and hide? Well I'm glad to tell you, it's all still deep within us just like those great memories I just awakened in you. I'm sure every now and again you may surprise yourself with what you come up with. But, unfortunately, it has been covered over by all that programming and indoctrination by human-made institutions you have visited, no fault of your own it's just part of the programming culture that we're living in.

Just like a strong fog where you can't see what direction you are headed in, it will blow over and just like the phoenix which will rise from the ashes, your creativity will burn bright once more, and your destiny and path will magically appear before your very eyes.

> No bird soars too high, if he soars with his own wings.
> – WILLIAM BLAKE

THE EDUCATION SYSTEM

Unfortunately, going through the education system as a young child and teenager, the majority of people are educated out of their creativity. During my schooling years, we were told to analyse, research, be rational and study our text books to get good grades and go onto further education.

If you couldn't go on any further you were seen as less competent, it's a great way to make people feel good about themselves! All of this type of thinking focused on the left side of the brain by the way, and it became habit and then a modern day ritual of behaviour.

Research has shown that most children, before they enter school, are ranked as being highly creative. By the time children are aged seven and above, only one-tenth of these children ranked as highly creative. This is due to our education system placing more emphasis on left brain skills. By the time we reach adulthood, only two percent of the Australian population ranks as being highly creative.

> The difficulty is that we do not make a world of our own, but fall into institutions already made.
> – RALPH WALDO EMERSON

There are a large percentage of the top 500 richest people in the world who have never made it to high school let alone university. But you will find with happy successful people, they are so creative and passionate and have a strong ability to come up with innovative ways to excel in their fields they are using both sides of the brain all the time.

> Nature has not said to me, "Be not poor" still less, "Be rich."
> She calls out to me, "Be independent."
> – NICOLAS DE CHAMFORT

We get driven away from our talents on the grounds that if the subjects are art, drama, music (all right hand brain hemisphere functions), they are not as useful as more academic subjects, and once you finish school, you may not find work or be able to make a living. But study Maths, English and Science, do well and you'll get admitted into university, do well, find a well paid job, earn lots of money and live a happy life. This is a myth. Our education system is, in general, more focused on our young ones getting good grades that will lead to university and a good job, to increase material possessions, not necessarily inner fulfilment and genuine happiness.

Creativity was generally not valued at school, only good grades were, so what's the outcome? People don't use their creative skills to their advantage in everyday life to achieve and overcome challenges that they face.

As children we are so driven to express ourselves, our abilities and talents that we constantly seek new ways of expressing our creativity and being unique in the environment that surrounds us. However, because we just don't interact with our friends, but also our parents, teachers and other young children, we become influenced by them, their values and beliefs and are instructed what to do, what to say, how to behave, and in my day — to be seen and not heard.

These interactions, both physically in our environment, and mentally, become hard wired into our little brains, and we become very susceptible to being told how to think and to not think for ourselves.

When we are young we are very vulnerable to being programmed by those we see as superior and look up to, such as parents and teachers. The self-defeating and self-limiting behaviour that people have today is a result of early programming and false memories that you accepted as true and correct, which were actually wrong, and have since stifled your creativity and your potential to be all that you can be.

Make the time to ask your children questions which will help them find happiness and inner fulfilment. Understand you don't own your children, they are not your possessions; they belong to the source, to God, to the Universe. They come through you, but are not from you. You are their guardians, mentors, their teachers, but only for a short cycle of time. Encourage them to be the best they can be. They are unique

Let the creativity flow

and individual souls. Don't limit their visions, make them dream and tell them they can do anything they want, inspire them. Let your children think for themselves and become independent as soon as possible, so they can learn to listen to themselves and use their own intuition. Ask your children the following:

- What activity makes you happy?
- What are you passionate about?
- What do you like to do that excites you?
- How can I help?

MY TEACHER

When I was in primary school, I had a teacher who cared enough to know I was having trouble at home, due to the fact I had tears in my eyes each day I came to school. This grade five teacher was also my coach in cricket, a sport of which I was an avid player. One morning, while the other students were doing their work in class, he called me to his desk to show me illustrations of how to correctly fast bowl a cricket ball. This kind act on a tough morning was like sunshine on a rainy day.

My teacher also used to make me go to the blackboard, in front of all the students in the classroom, and work out long division, even when the other children would laugh or snigger at me, as maths was not one of my strengths. Although I was embarrassed at the time, it also showed me that he cared about me, and made me feel important. On the next maths exam, I aced it by getting 100%, beating all the more intelligent students who laughed at me. As it turned out, I also got a hat-trick at the next cricket match against a rival school.

To Mr Peter Hose, thank you for making me feel important and taking the time to support, encourage and strengthen my inner talents. You lit the spark within me, my friend. You showed me that I mattered.

To all the teachers reading this, please make sure you encourage all your students, make them feel important, because your motivation and guidance will show them that they all matter and they can do anything they put their minds to, just like I have.

The young are not vessels to be filled; they are fires to be lit.
– PLUTARCH

CHANGE IS COMING

All your previous programming and thought patterns are about to change today, because the brain has the power to download new programs at such a rapid rate you can change the way you think and feel. You can change your beliefs about who you are and what you were told, to new ways of thinking and acting. When we provide the brain with new positive neurological pathways, it will give rise to new mental activity. Every time we have new experiences, moments of happiness and success, we are in fact, creating new neuron pathways to bring about new opportunities and a more creative way of living and changing our realities into something fun and innovative.

By making sure we use our creativity, the neural pathways that carry this information will always be strengthened and in use so those connections of the brain will always be available to us. Remember this, "The neurons that fire together, wire together."

Let go of your self-limiting and self-defeating thinking because this is not who you are. Change the program of your life or others will program you.

There is a term where, when the brain rewires itself automatically through our intentions of change from negative conscious thoughts, actions, behaviour, rituals and habits to positive ones, it's called Neuroplasticity. So when you direct your intentions, positive or negative, it gets hardwired by neurons in the brain.

Be positive, make sure you activate your will and imagination towards a particular purpose. Direct your creativity for good in your life and let it manifest itself today. Any pattern of emotion and behaviour that is continually reinforced will become a voluntary and programmed response, it's called the law of reinforcement.

> Resolve to be thyself; and know, that he who
> finds himself, loses his misery.
> — MATTHEW ARNOLD

Human-made institutions make people learn and behave a certain way and let you know what they expect from you until you conform to their rules and regulations. People turn into 'sheeple'. It's called following the herd mentality. Picasso said, "All children are born artists, the problem is to remain artists as we grow up." So true!

This mentality goes into the workplace as well. Try and form an opinion of your own that differs from senior management and see how far you get in your career. You'll be deemed a trouble maker or someone that will have to be watched by management, as I have experienced this in my own life, many years ago.

MY FRIENDS

A couple of friends of mine from school were seen as different and unconventional because they were always asking questions that were deemed inappropriate. They were always coming up with new ideas and different ways outside the norm to do assignments, but were told to stick by the rules and policy of school assessment or be marked as incompetent.

My friends were creative and I admired them for that. They weren't afraid of making mistakes and being wrong, they knew to come up with anything original you're going to make mistakes, it's all a part of the creative and learning process.

By the time we have become adults we don't want to make mistakes, it's a big no-no isn't it! "Oh, who made the mistake, what a stupid mistake that is," "Who's the idiot that did that?"

No wonder no-one wants to stand out from the crowd and try anything different, become creative and enjoy their talents. That's the mentality of it all. How are we supposed to be creative and innovative when limited value is placed on creativity in the education system and society in general? How can we learn from our mistakes if we feel foolish by making them in the first place?

> All life is an experiment, the more experiments you make the better.
> – RALPH WALDO EMERSON

My friends are now doing well for themselves in their chosen fields of work, they are wealthy and happy, and didn't go to university. They kept their creativity flowing and channelled it through their everyday lives, in their careers, relationships, family and with their children. They enjoy being successful and contributing to their community. They didn't let themselves be conditioned to live in their heads; they weren't educated out of being creative. They followed their dreams and ideas, they dared to be original. Do you?

CREATIVE INFLUENCES

Where would our society be today without the creative and influential people who have contributed and thought outside the box? Just to name a few: Albert Einstein, Thomas Edison, Orville and Wilbur Wright (the Wright Brothers), Louise Hay, Richard Branson, Henry Ford, Bill Gates, Leonardo Da Vinci, William Shakespeare and Oprah Winfrey. Makes you wonder doesn't it? These are the people who have changed our society by understanding the creative process.

When we listen to the world within (our intuition) we are able to grasp the grand ideals of beauty, power, and wisdom and realise we can develop and express these ideals in the outside world. This will be for the greater good and we will be in harmony with everyone and everything. This is when magic happens and creativity manifests itself. To all those that seek it, it is available to you. Be daring, be bold, be courageous.

> To the dull mind all nature is leader. To the illumined mind, the whole world burns and sparkles with light.
> — RALPH WALDO EMERSON

Remember this, it's not money that keeps our society going, breaking new barriers of innovation and ingenuity, and making us progress. All the money in the world isn't enough it would only last for so long. It's great thinkers who have tuned in and opened their minds to keep us at the forefront of new technologies, inventions and creativity. It's the ability to think with good intentions implied that keeps society moving forward. Money is just a by-product of those people who tap into the creativity and use their minds for the greater good.

> Who looks outside dreams; who looks inside wakes.
> — CARL JUNG

RECLAIM YOUR CREATIVITY

Ok, are you ready to reclaim your creativity and open your mind? Are you going to use your imagination, become more innovative, original and alive with spontaneity, excitement and open the door to new possibilities? Let go of old rituals that aren't giving you the life you know you deserve and desire. Be prepared to make mistakes and know that it's a process of learning and growing, to evolve into the new you.

Let the creativity flow

> Deep down within the core of our being, lies a creative power, the capacity to create what is to be, and the urge to make unremitting efforts until we have given it shape in one way or another, either outside ourselves or within our own person.
> – JOHANN WOLFGANG VON GOETHE

Start seeing people in a new light, do things differently, throw away the old habits and behaviours that don't work for you. Look around, are you happy?

Change your routine. Get back your individuality, step out of the norm, and be unique. See your life through the eyes of a child, be stress free, be here now and listen to your ideas, try them all until you find one that works. Make mistakes and don't be afraid, this is how we challenge ourselves and progress forward. The more ideas you have, the greater the odds you have of achieving happiness and success for yourself. Let your imagination run wild. If you have a role model or somebody you admire, ask yourself, what would they do in your position or situation?

There are so many sources of information; we are living today in the most technologically advanced society ever of the human race. Don't be afraid to ask people who can help you, people love to help and usually don't mind giving up their time, people like to feel needed and valued.

This is how you open up your consciousness to let the creativity flow and connect with infinite intelligence. Ask as many questions as possible, just like a child would, they don't care what other people think; they're not critical of themselves. Remember, there are no dumb questions the only stupid question is the one that never gets asked.

Be an adventurer in your life, like when you were a child exploring and discovering new methods and ways to go about your projects and daily life. Make your life fun.

> Life must be lived as play.
> – PLATO

VISUALISE TALKING TO GREAT MINDS

Converse with people who have passed on (I like to call it graduated) who you have admired throughout history, Eleanor Roosevelt,

Churchill, Socrates, Lincoln, Einstein, just to name a few.

To do this, visualise and use your imagination to talk to them and ask for their advice. Napoleon Hill explains in his book *Think and Grow Rich*, how he used to imagine having meetings with invisible counsellors, as he would call them.

He asked advice from great people such as Lincoln and Ford and others that he looked up to, for advice on how to solve problems, generate new ideas, as well as ways to overcome challenges he was facing in his life.

I recommend you read his book when you get the chance, it was the first human potential book that really moved me, and today is a classic.

LET GO OF PROGRAMMING

Let go of your programming, believe you are creative, breathe it, visualise it, affirm it and live it, act like you're creative and guess what, you will become creative consciousness. The people who believe they are creative in life, are. And the people who don't believe they are, won't be.

Your thoughts create your reality and how you live your life. Whatever you focus on, it expands. You will receive what you put out into the energy web. This is the law of attraction, the law of cause and effect. Quantum physics tells us that we're living in a big bowl of energy and everything is connected. Mystics have been saying this since the dawn of time, science has just caught up. It's time to discover oneness with energy and let it work for you in your life with the best intentions.

RELAX

What is the one thing that helps you relax? I suggest you do this. When you're relaxed, you're in the moment and you have no stress. It can be taking the dog for a walk, running, swimming at the beach, fishing. This is when you get your best ideas and your intuition talks to you. It can come to you as a little inner voice, or a hunch, it happens when you're connected and are tapping into the storeroom of endless possibility.

Listen to your Solar Plexus, your third chakra, it will help you by giving you that gut feeling of surety. It is here you connect with the infinite intelligence and get the correct answers to put you on your path.

> Cease striving; then there will be self transformation.
> – CHUANG-TSE

CREATIVITY STRATEGIES

Listed below are some simple strategies to help boost your creativity.

- Meditate daily to still your mind.
- Carry a note book to write down your thoughts, feelings and any other creative ideas as they come to you.
- Surround yourself and be influenced by other creative people.
- Discover yourself through artistic expression such as painting, pottery, drawing, or even cake decorating.
- Take up a hobby that you enjoy to put you in the moment and still your mind, such as cooking, photography, gardening, dancing, sewing or fishing.

Mozart said his musical ideas came to him when he was by himself or during the night when he couldn't sleep. When our mind is still we can tap into our inner self, the source of our creativity.

If you have children or know someone with a child, encourage them to embrace their creativity and to develop it and strengthen it. Make sure you tell them how creative they are. Positive reinforcement for children and teenagers is like giving water to a person who has been out in the desert for a few days, they need it desperately. Don't let your children be disempowered by the system, let them follow their dreams, don't put a blanket over their imaginations, let them grow. Let their lights forever burn brightly.

Positive self-belief in your creative abilities will last a lifetime. It's time to be creative, get inspired by art or nature, be unique and an individual, celebrate your independence, escape mediocrity and let your creativity flow.

Creativity takes courage.
– HENRI MATISSE

NINE
Question time

> The important thing is not to stop questioning; curiosity has its own reason for existing. One cannot help but be in awe when contemplating the mysteries of eternity, of life, of the marvellous structure of reality. It is enough if one tries merely to comprehend a little of the mystery everyday. The important thing is to never stop questioning. Never lose a holy curiosity.
> – ALBERT EINSTEIN

This chapter focuses on questions which I have included so you can ask questions about your own life. Questions such as, "Am I happy with my life", "What am I doing with it and the people who I share it with?" I truly believe it's time for you to ask the big questions in your life. Are you ready for this?

Asking questions can be a valuable tool in the process of self-discovery, which will enhance your life. By becoming familiar with your strengths and weaknesses, positives and negatives, you'll come to an 'a-ha' moment which will bridge the gap for you, and get you moving towards a more rewarding life.

By filling the gaps in your life, you'll build on a much stronger foundation for happiness and success. If any of these questions make you feel disappointed or frustrated or angry, that's a good thing. Embrace these feelings, they will give you the motivation to make changes in your life as well as the drive to make the improvement you need to live the life you want for yourself. I have noticed that successful people in life always ask better questions, which create a better quality of life.

By answering all of these questions truthfully you will be opening your mind to a new level of consciousness. By becoming more aware of your life and who you are, you're taking the most important step of your journey to self-transformation and a life worth living.

> Our grand business undoubtebly is, not to see what lies dimly at a distance, but to do what lies clearly at hand.
> – THOMAS CARLYLE

QUESTIONS

Answer the following questions with deep thought and honesty. Be true to yourself and ensure you are not rushing through them; take time and ponder your thoughts.

Some space has been provided for your answers below, however you may wish to use a notebook, which can be useful to also write down your feelings and emotions as they come up.

> He that cannot ask, cannot live.
> – OLD PROVERB

YOUR LIFE

Are you happy in your life, in general? _____

Do you think you could improve your life? _____

In what areas? Please list _____

_____

What will make your happier? _____

_____

Are you satisfied with your life? If not, why? _____

_____

Write down five things you're grateful for in your life

1 _____
2 _____
3 _____
4 _____
5 _____

> I cried because I had no shoes, until I met a man who had no feet.
> – PERSIAN SAYING

Always appreciate what you have in your life. Don't take anything for granted. Life is very precious. When you're grateful you'll enjoy high levels of emotional and physical well-being, in the now.

> Happiness is the meaning and the purpose of life,
> the whole aim and end of human existence.
> – ARISTOTLE

Discover Your Path

List three things that give you meaning
1
2
3
List three things that give you pleasure
1
2
3
What do you believe is your calling or purpose in your life?

The first answer that comes to you from your heart is the one you want to listen to. Don't over-analyse your thoughts.

It's time to commit to reducing your rat race life and dedicating yourself to things that give you meaning and purpose. So you can truly understand who it is that you really are.

What are you doing to improve your life?

How are you spending most of your day?

Does this make you happy?

What could you do more of in your life?

What could you do less of in your life?

> A man sooner or later discovers that he is the master gardener of his soul, the director of his life.
> – JAMES ALLEN

Do you feel like you live in tomorrow land?

Question time

What are the things you procrastinate about in your life? ⎯⎯⎯

Is living life like this working for you? ⎯⎯⎯

What are you doing to change this? ⎯⎯⎯

> If you don't change directions, you'll end up where you are heading.
> – LAO TZU

WELL BALANCED LIFE

The majority of people only have just enough time; we generally live a busy lifestyle these days with competing priorities and commitments. In doing so, we tend to only concentrate on one or two facets of our lives. Usually they are work or relationships. If one or both of these fail, they become depressed, empty and bored and have no real meaning or purpose. To be a well-rounded person, you must work on all different areas of your life to make you fulfilled and satisfied, and your inner well full of spiritual goodness.

Please circle below the different areas of your life that apply to you at this moment. Once you have circled those that are applicable to you, place a rating of 1 to 10 (1 meaning empty and 10 meaning fulfilled) in this component of your life.

Charity / community	⎯⎯ [RATING]
Family connections	⎯⎯ [RATING]
Friends	⎯⎯ [RATING]
Healthy eating	⎯⎯ [RATING]
Hobby / artistic pursuits	⎯⎯ [RATING]
Leisure	⎯⎯ [RATING]
Money	⎯⎯ [RATING]
Regular exercise	⎯⎯ [RATING]
Rest and relaxation	⎯⎯ [RATING]
Self-development	⎯⎯ [RATING]
Travel	⎯⎯ [RATING]

Now you have circled and rated those components, for those that are not circled — what are you going to do to start to improving these areas of your life? Please monitor your progress in each facet of your life every few months.

> Self conquest is the greatest of victories.
> — PLATO

AWAKENING EXERCISE

Choosing from the descriptions in the list below, select which one best describes you? Please circle. You can circle more than one category as there are no right or wrong answers.

Hedonist — you focus on the present while ignoring the potential negative consequences of your actions.   Y   N

Rat racer — you suffer now for the purpose of some anticipated gain.   Y   N

Nihilist — You have lost lust for life and you don't enjoy the moment, are a slave to the past. So you have no sense of future purpose.   Y   N

Realist — You have your feet firmly on the ground and life is either black or white and no shades of grey.   Y   N

Idealist — A dreamer who devotes time to a calling and a purpose.   Y   N

This is an awakening exercise if you don't like what you see with your answers and it doesn't feel right, change it.

Don't let society's programming, labelling and indoctrination dictate what a meaningful life means to you. You must choose your purpose in accordance with your own values, meanings and passions, rather than conforming to others expectations. Your life must be self-generated and come from deep within, your very essence, your soul and have a real significance to you and only you.

> The great and glorious masterpiece of man is to live with purpose.
> — MICHEL DE MONTAIGNE

TIME MANAGEMENT

How often do you say, "I don't have enough time?" _____

Do you think it's about time you prioritise your time a lot better? _____

Do you make a list of all the important tasks you need to do at the beginning of your day or before you finish your day's work?
If no, why not? _____

Are you time affluent? Meaning, do you have time for the activities that give you meaning and pleasure? _____

Do you feel time poverty? Do you feel you are constantly stressed and rushed to get things done throughout your day? _____

> **You must make your intentions concrete!**
>
> Plan your time according to your dreams, not according to your watch.
> — *UNKNOWN*

WORK LIFE AND CAREER

Do you look forward to the start of your day? _____
Do you enjoy your work? _____
Does it make you happy and fulfilled? _____
Do you think you're using your full potential in the workplace? If not, why? And what are you doing today to change this? _____

What have you learnt or studied lately or what skills have you acquired to better yourself for the future? _____

Action is the key to success.

Discover Your Path

STRENGTHS

What are your strengths? List five below.

1
2
3
4
5

What are you doing to develop these?

> As long as habit and routine dictate the pattern of living new dimensions of the soul will not emerge.
> – HENRY VAN DYKE

COMFORT ZONE

> All things change, yet we need not fear anything new.
> – MARCUS AURELIUS

Do you live in either a state of fear or anxiety?

Does this keep you in your comfort zone?

Is this working for you in your life?

What are you doing to change this?

> What need is there of fear, since it is your power to inquire what ought to be done.
> – MARCUS AURELIUS

List five dysfunctional beliefs about yourself that keeps your potential immobilised.

1 _____
2 _____
3 _____
4 _____
5 _____

> Things do not change; we change.
> – HENRY DAVID THOREAU

List five destructive habits or behaviours that keep you from moving forward in your life.

1 _____
2 _____
3 _____
4 _____
5 _____

Now list five things that you're going to do today to change these beliefs, habits and behaviours to make you feel constructive and that you're participating in your life for a better tomorrow.

1 _____
2 _____
3 _____
4 _____
5 _____

People are programmed by society and culture not to believe in themselves.

OUTLOOK ON LIFE

Would you describe yourself as a positive or negative person, in general?

_____
_____

Could you improve this outlook?

Have you ever monitored your thoughts to see how positive or negative you are? (Refer to chapter seven for an exercise to help you)

Begin this today and make a change if necessary. It's a change worth doing. Your future life depends on it!

> Always the beautiful answer who asks a more beautiful question.
> — E. E CUMMINGS

CHANGE

Do you want change in one or more aspects of your life?

What are the consequences if you don't change?

Are you willing to make sacrifices?

What are they?

> I find it fascinating that most people plan their vacations with better care than they plan their lives. Perhaps that is because escape is easier than change.
> — JIM ROHN

TALENTS AND ABILITIES

What are your unique gifts, talents and abilities?

Are you using them to your best advantage?

What do you really enjoy in your life, what makes you lose track of time?

Question time

When you listen to your heart what does it tell you to do? _____

Do you have the courage to follow it? _____

If you had all the money in the world and all time in the world what would you be doing? _____

> When all the emotions of the body have become rhythmical the body has, as it were, a gigantic battery of will.
> – UNKNOWN

HEALTH AND BODY

Do you exercise regularly? _____

If not, why? _____

Do you eat nutritious food daily? _____

Do you like the way you look and feel? _____

If not, what are you doing about it? _____

Are you as healthy as you want to be? _____

What are you doing about this? _____

Do you treat your body as a temple? _____

Do you have addictions? _____

What are you doing to eliminate these from your life?

> Take precautions before evil appears;
> regulate things before disorder has begun.
> — LAO-TSE

GOALS

Do you set short, medium and long term goals for things that are important to you?

If your answer was no, why?

What is the barrier stopping you from pursuing your goals?

Do you want direction in your life?	◯ Y ◯ N
Do you want meaning in your life?	◯ Y ◯ N
Do you want purpose in your life?	◯ Y ◯ N
Do you feel the need to express your inner needs?	◯ Y ◯ N
Do you feel you need happiness and enjoyment in the present?	◯ Y ◯ N
Do you want to feel liberated in the here and now?	◯ Y ◯ N
Do you have a destination to focus on in your life?	◯ Y ◯ N

If you answered yes to two or more of these questions about goals, you need to write down your goals and work on achieving them. You can revisit chapter five for help to write and achieve your goals.

> People with goals have success because they know where they're going.
> — EARL NIGHTINGALE

THOUGHT PROCESS

Please circle the thought process below that best describes how you think.

All-or-nothing — you only see black or white and don't recognise the shades of grey in between.

Disregarding the positive — you turn positive experiences into negative experiences.

Emotional reasoning — you use your emotions to guide your truth, (even if they are negative emotions), which may mislead you taking the appropriate action.

Labelling — you tend to put a label on yourself and others, which is mostly negative, such as, "He's a loser", "I'm not good enough".

Magnification and minimisation — you highlight the negative (such as insecurities and fears) and ignore the important, more positive things such as your strengths.

Mental filter — you tend to only focus on the negative and ignore the positive information.

Overgeneralisation — you draw inference from a previous event in your life and apply it to other events, even if they are unrelated.

What are you going to do to improve these thoughts processes in your life? ___

RELATIONSHIPS

*No person is your friend who demands your silence
or denies your right to grow.
– ALICE WALKER*

Are you happy in your current relationship? ___

Are your emotional and physical needs being met with your partner? ___

Do you have many friends? ___

Are you connected to them on a deeper level? ___

Do you encourage your partner to be all they can be? ○ Y ○ N
If you answered no, why? ___

Discover Your Path

Do you bring out the best in your partner? ◯ Y ◯ N
Do you control and manipulate your partner? ◯ Y ◯ N
If you answered yes, why? _____

Are you attached or dependent on your partner's happiness?

If you answered yes, why? _____

Do you give your partner space to be themselves? ◯ Y ◯ N

If you answered no, why? _____

Do you think it's time to reclaim your independence in your relationship? ◯ Y ◯ N

What are you going to do to reclaim your independence in your relationship with your partner? _____

There are no right or wrong answers here. As difficult as it can be, you need to answer these questions truthfully and honestly. To bring about an awareness of what parts of your relationship need working on, discuss with your partner. If you need assistance working through issues, a qualified relationship counsellor can help.

> In any relationships in which two people become one,
> the end result is two half people.
> – DR WAYNE W DYER

PERSONAL VALUES

Do you treat people the way you want to be treated? _____

Are you respectful of yourself and others?

Are you a kind and friendly person?

Do you have good values and morals?

Are you more into superficial needs and wants than making deeper connections with people?

Are you genuine and authentic?

Do you have honour?

Do you listen to, encourage or participate in gossip? If so, why? This is destructive behaviour.

Do you break your word? If you do, it's time to change.

> Kindness is the language in which the deaf
> can hear and the blind can see.
> — MARK TWAIN

MONEY

> Charity and personal force are the only investments worth anything.
> — WALT WHITMAN

What are you doing to make yourself more valuable to the marketplace?

Are you happy with the wage or salary you earn?

If not, what are you doing about it to change your circumstances?

Do you want to provide more money for yourself and your loved ones?

If so, what have you done to make it so?

Have you been taking night classes, going to college, university or workshops to better yourself and your financial prospects?

What would you really like to do to make a living?

> Success is not the key to happiness, happiness is the key to success, if you love what you're doing, you will be successful.
> — ALBERT SCHWEITZER

MEDITATION

Do you meditate? Do you regularly do an activity that quietens your mind, and clears the mind chatter?

If you don't, please start. It will allow you to listen to your heart and have peace from within. It will change your life. This is very important — to me it is most important. Please start 10 to 15 minutes a day to begin with, and make this a positive habit every day. All the answers you seek will be revealed to you, with a clear and quiet mind. Simple meditation exercises are explained in chapter 10.

> Silence is the true friend that never betrays.
> — CONFUCIUS

DREAMS

When you're asleep you need your dreams, and when you're awake you need your dreams.

What are your dreams?

What are you doing to make them a reality?

What have you done recently in achieving your dreams? _____

How much time do you take out of your day for this? _____

Are you committed to your dreams? _____

Are you using excuses right now? _____

To have your dreams come true, you must become a dreamer. Believe and it will happen.

That's great; you have finished the questionnaire exercise. The purpose was to highlight to you questions that you may not ask yourself in your day to day living. By asking yourself these questions, it puts your life into perspective. It makes you focus on what needs your attention. By doing this, you can have an action plan, sink your teeth into what needs to be done, bring about change and growth and live a happier, healthier, more balanced, more fulfilled life. Don't you think it's time you started living the life that you truly desire? I know you do! So, get out there and do it!

> Dream as if you will live forever
> Live as if you will die today.
> – JAMES DEAN

TEN
Are you listening?

> To a mind that is still, the whole universe surrenders.
> — CHUANG TSE

In my life I have always followed my heart and listened to my intuition. I can honestly say I have always trusted and had faith in my closest friend and confidant. It has always given me the inner wisdom and knowledge that logical and analytical thought couldn't bring to the table. There was always a gap that couldn't be filled but my inner voice could make me see truth clearly in my everyday decisions. To me, there's strength and a sense of freedom knowing my intuition would have exactly what I was looking for when I most needed it. You must look deep within yourself to find what you want out of life.

> The thoughts that come often unsought, and, as it were, drop into the mind, are commonly the most valuable of any we have.
> — JOHN LOCKE

When we're tapping into our intuition the right hemisphere of our brains are being used. The right side of the brain is accessed for creativity, it works best at expressive and creative tasks, including the music we listen to, the colours we wear, the symbols in our dreams and around us, remembering faces we have seen and retrieving names. This side of the brain is where we unlock the subconscious mind and all the beliefs and programs we have developed since childhood.

Our dreams come from the subconscious mind into our consciousness when we're asleep. It's the mystical place within, where great people throughout history have received their inspiration. Marie Curie, Mozart, Einstein, Edison, Socrates, Henry Ford, Gates, Branson and many more talented and gifted people have stated that intuition had been the key ingredient to their success.

The subconscious part of us is where all our true selves' natural talents are waiting to be discovered, just like hidden treasure. You must be prepared to consult your subconscious mind, to know who you really are.

It blows my mind how much we take in consciously, with our everyday experiences, thoughts and knowledge of what we have learnt throughout our development as people. But it's the (unconscious) subconscious and right hemisphere of the brain where we can access the infinite library of information. Your intuition is how you tap into it. And it is here where the truth to all of your questions about life and all its mysteries and wonder can be found. You must dare to listen to yourself and your feelings; here you'll find your truth. Mystics and holy men have been doing this since the dawn of time and now you can too.

It can come as a voice, a sense, a knowing, a feeling, a hunch and a gut instinct. When we're children we know automatically if we like someone or not, if they're friendly or hostile. We are born with this inner radar, and we trust that it's in full operating order and have the courage to follow the mysterious and the hidden. This is the road less travelled, do you dare?

> What lies behind us and what lies before us,
> are tiny compared to what lies within us.
> – RALPH WALDO EMERSON

The majority of people stop listening and trusting themselves for something more real and tangible, something they can see and touch. As we grow up many people stop expressing how they feel and suppress their emotions out of fear of being judged by family and friends. We don't want to be seen as weak and vulnerable and be put on the outside of a group, where we can have an open target on our backs.

Even in school, we don't get taught to listen and feel for the answers, but to look for knowledge and facts out of text books. The mind thinks and the body feels, remember we're energetic beings, how can you go against what you feel? It's going against who you are.

LISTEN TO YOUR INTUITION

But to live accordingly to our higher purpose we must listen to our intuition as we can never get all the cold hard facts and information we need at the time to make the appropriate decisions. There's always a gap isn't there, between making the right or wrong decision? At some stage of the process we must go with what feels right to us and inquire within. Understanding your feelings are the facts. Your feelings don't lie to you. Have you ever been wrong when you listened to your feelings? It's time to take advice from your inner sage and do what's right for you!

> As he thinketh in his heart, so is he.
> — PROVERBS 23:7

LISTEN TO YOUR HEART

Starting today, I want you to listen more to your heart and emotions. Our emotions and feelings are the real language of our soul talking to us and guiding us every step of the way. If you want the truth and you start to over-rationalise and become too analytical and logical, ask your intuition to make sure you feel right about the decision. You do this by asking questions like, "How do I feel about this?", "How will this make me feel if I go ahead and do this?", "Does this feel right for me?" Listen to your first impulse, it will be subtle. Do you feel good about it or does it make you feel sick in the stomach? These are yes and no answers.

> Errors, like straws, upon the surface flow;
> he who would reach for pearls must dive below.
> — JOHN DRYDEN

It may not be as direct as this. It might not come as quickly as this, maybe later on when you're doing something else and when you least expect it. Watch out for fleeting images, symbols, words or senses that you can individually recognise as your own particular truth. Sometimes for me, it may come in a lyric of a song or a conversation I have with a friend, but most of the time it's when I'm in solitude and I'm left alone to ponder. I get my best ideas and receive the answers to the question my mind can't answer for me.

It's very important to be honest with yourself, trust and stick by your inner convictions. Take responsibility for yourself and express what you feel, otherwise if you let other people's attitudes and behaviours control you, you will end up in situations that you didn't want to end up in. These may include dead end relationships, jobs, friendships and any other scenarios where you may be harmed, energetically, mentally, spiritually, emotionally or physically.

> As soon as you trust yourself, you will know how to live.
> — JOHANN WOLFGANG VON GOETHE

STOP JUDGING YOURSELF

Until you stop judging, blaming and sabotaging yourself, life will keep giving you more of the same. You must take responsibility and take the appropriate action. Let go of all mind interpretation, don't over-analyse so much, or be too logical, get out of your head and listen to your heart. Detach from your ego so you can listen and recognise your intuition sending you messages from within.

LET GO OF LABELS

Let go of labels and your identification, and let your soul speak to you through your heart. Until then, history will repeat itself starting off as a small challenge and ending up as a disaster. Then you have to deal with it head on. These are the consequences we face if we're not truthful to ourselves and try and live out someone else's expectations and hopes for us.

Have you ever said, "I did it for you", or "I did it to make you happy"? I say to you, make yourself happy, do the right thing that fulfils you, and never let someone else have that control and power over you. It lets them squash and hinder your full potential and lower your self-worth and confidence. Don't disempower yourself to keep other people happy — you're better than this. Listen to yourself; you have all the answers within. Enlightenment comes when you trust yourself and are independent of other's opinions and actions.

LISTEN TO YOUR BODY

If you're not following your intuition and are going against your own true wishes, your body will talk to you through aches and pains throughout your body. Aches and pains are like a lighthouse on top of a cliff warning you that there's danger nearby and that you need to take the appropriate action not to hit the rocks and run into trouble.

You have to be true to yourself and trust yourself and your inner wisdom. Ask your body or the part of your body where the imbalance is and ask why you're sore there and what you need to do to unblock the energy flow and restore balance. Listen for your answer as it will come to you. Have the courage to ask and have patience. A holistic health practitioner can also help you identify the body/mind connection of your aches and pains and what you must do to restore balance within yourself.

YOUR INTUITION HAS NO EGO

Remember, there is no fear or ego in intuition. Your intuition operates in the now; it doesn't listen to your conditioning or programming. That's why so many people have trouble following it. You need to let go and trust. When you do this, you will know by the way you feel spiritually, physically, emotionally and energetically. You will feel lighter so the frequency of your body will vibrate higher, your body will have more flexibility and mobility and be free of pain. Your self-worth will be higher, you'll want to be treated with respect and love and you'll give it in return without any harps or gripes and you'll see the beauty and the wonder in everyone and everything.

Everything you do throughout the day will fall into place; everything will run smoothly and effortlessly. This is what is called flow, like you're in the zone, and you can see things before and after they happen and everything you do is being done at the right time and place and you get a true inner fulfilment of happiness. This is where time doesn't exist because you're in the now. Does that sound like a nice way to live? Sounds beautiful to me and I know you will soon experience this!

At one time or another we all have experienced the use of our intuition in our lives. It can come with a phone call and before you pick up the phone you know who it is. Or, you think about a friend you haven't seen in a while and you pick up the phone to call them to find out they're not well. Perhaps you were at a party and could feel someone staring at you, and you turn around to catch someone's eye? These are just a few examples of intuition and how we experience it in our lives. Now that I have explained to you what it is and what intuition can do for you, it's time to develop it and strengthen it.

> The only tyrant I accept in this world is the 'still small voice' within.
> – MAHATMA GANDHI

MEDITATION

Solitude and silence are some key ingredients to listening to the voice within. Meditation has been practiced for thousands of years. It can be a terrific way to quiet the mind and get all the noise and raciness to slow down to be able to listen to your intuition.

Eastern mystics call this mind noise 'monkey chatter'. Meditation to me, is the stilling of one's mind through the focus of the breath. It's a great way for people who suffer from depression, anxiety and who are uptight and need to let go and relax. The benefits will be outstanding when you meditate and let go from within.

BENEFITS OF MEDITATION

I found in my daily life, through the benefits of meditation, that I have become more relaxed physically and mentally. I have better movement and my headaches disappear. I am calmer and don't react to challenges or obstacles that would usually get me bent out of shape. I feel more serene and at peace with myself and am able to go with the flow, respond to life and not react to it. Solutions to life's challenges come much easier to me; my sense of self-worth is much more evident as I don't have to live up to or measure up to anybody's expectations of me. I have a true understanding that whatever comes my way I have the knowledge and inner wisdom to handle it, just by listening and trusting myself. Soon you'll have a mind that is open and attached to nothing. There is no attachment to intuition, only your truth.

A SIMPLE MEDITATION

Sit upright in a comfortable chair with your back up against the back support with your feet shoulder width apart.

Shut your eyes and put the tip of your tongue touching the roof of your mouth.

Now, I want you to visualise a golden light around your body to cleanse your aura.

Picture a golden shaft of light going through the top part of your head and cleansing the inside of your body of any ill health, aches or pains.

Now visualise the soles of your feet growing roots like a tree to ground you to mother earth for stability.

Through your nostrils breathe in nice and deeply, into the pit of your stomach, feeling your chest rise and expand.

And on the out breath, release all tension and stress out of your body, feeling lighter and stress free. Let your thoughts come and go like waves on an ocean, but pay no attention to them.

Continue practising meditation for about 10 to 15 minutes initially and gradually increase the time each day.

NO SET RULES FOR MEDITATION

There are no set rules for meditation. You don't have to be in a room with candles and birds of the forest music to get the benefits of meditation. This may help some people set the mood and create a relaxing atmosphere, but it's not for everyone. Start out with 10 to 15 minutes each day, and make sure there are no distractions. Take the phone off the hook or put your mobile on silent. Persistence is the key here and try to do it the same time every day to make it a good ritual for you.

Don't give up, give it time. Soon, you'll want to do it for longer, and take it to thirty minutes. Whatever works for you, as we are all different. If you miss a day or two just get back to it and pick it up where you left off. The more times you do it the sooner you'll get into a tranquil state. This is how you know you're progressing. Let your thoughts come and go and a sense of peace and calm will come over you. This is a great exercise to strengthen your intuitive ability — give it time. However, please do it.

MEDITATION COMES IN MANY FORMS

The majority of people are in a meditative state throughout the day, when they are focusing on one thing at a time. Meditation can come in many forms. It can be when you're doing the washing up, the gardening, in the gym, going for a walk, swimming in the ocean, or playing your favourite sport or enjoying your hobby.

When you're in the now, focusing on one thing at a time, that's meditation. This is when you'll receive your best ideas and impressions, this is when you're relaxed, stress free and are open to receive the gifts of inspiration and confidence when you're open, and haven't got three or four other things going on in your mind at the same time.

> Just by listening deeply we alleviate pain and suffering.
> – BUDDHIST SAYING

SWITCH YOUR PEN HAND

An exercise to strengthen the right side of your brain is to put your pen in the opposite of your dominant hand. So, if you're right handed, write left hand and visa versa. It will be weird at first, but give it time and ask yourself questions in regards to the challenges you are currently facing. This is also called automatic writing, where you can tune into your higher self. Remember, practice makes improvement. Perfection doesn't exist, it's an egotistical trait and only leads to destructive thought patterns, beliefs and behaviours.

WRITE DOWN WHAT YOUR INTUITION SAYS

Listening to your intuition takes time and practice. Always be confident and receptive when asking your intuition for answers. Be positive and expect and deserve your intuition will give you the best possible answer for your soul's development, understanding and growth.

Your intuition can come to you when you least expect it, always have a small notepad and pen by your bedside table, in the car and in your wallet or purse. This is so you don't get distracted, forget, or lose forever what you're being told.

Importantly be open, have faith, trust in the process and have the courage to take action. Taking action on your intuition and having the courage to follow it will lead you down the path of enlightenment. Find inner peace within yourself because then you will live a life of freedom and fulfilment.

Take the journey from within, become a modern day mystic. Be still and listen within the silence, it is here your soul's secrets will be shared with you.

The people in this life who are happy and truly fulfilled inside themselves are the doers of this world not the gunners (those that are going to do). Which one are you? Are you listening now?

> It is true that knowledge is within ourselves, but this has to be called forth by another knowledge. Although the capacity to know is inside us, it must be called out.
> – SWAMI VIVEKANANDA

ELEVEN
Your temple

It is health that is real wealth and not pieces of gold and silver.
— MAHATMA GANDHI

MY PERSONAL JOURNEY

When I was fifteen, I can remember playing football at the park with my friends after school. There were two teams (shirts on and shirts off) and I was in the shirts off team. I was a flat chested and skinny young teenager. During this football match, my friend's sister sidled up beside me and said I was so thin that it looked like I hadn't eaten in six months. The hide on her I thought, if I can recall she was no fitness model!

WAKE UP CALL

This really hurt my feelings. I was a really shy, sensitive kid with no self-confidence whatsoever, and although I never took any notice of my physique (and who really does at this age, I know I didn't). But a cutting comment from this girl did make me become more aware of my physical appearance (self-image) and how other people judge you on appearances and label you. This was a wake up call for me that day — thanks for that.

As I became aware of my other team mate's bodies and measuring myself up against them I noticed that no two of my team mates were the same. We're all different shapes and sizes and we're all gifted with our parent's genetics, some good and not so good, it just comes down to your perception.

But, I can remember a new boy named Chris, who had just moved into the neighbourhood. To me he looked like a man trapped in a teenager's body. His chest was much thicker than everybody else's, his arms were as big as my average team mate's legs. With this physique I also noticed that Chris had more self-confidence and self esteem as well, and in turn, he treated people kindly and he respected himself and others as well.

As I became more aware of all of this, I could see the local girls were admiring and even swooning over him. All the while, I wanted to run away and hide. I was playing golf at the time and trust me you don't look like that by playing golf. My family lived about a minute away from a golf course. So that's the sport all my mates and I were into.

A NEW FRIEND AND EARLY GUIDE
The next day I was practising my golf in the park and Chris was throwing his javelin. At one stage the javelin came quite close to me so I went over and told Chris to be careful. He admired me for my courage and invited me to his house for lunch. We became friends.

Chris and I had many things in common including our tastebuds, as we were both from Sicilian heritage and fittingly, we had pasta for lunch. After lunch we went down into his garage and I saw this unusual looking bench with weights on a bar, he told me it was called a bench press for building up your chest muscles.

WEIGHTS PROGRAM
To me, it was like he was talking another language, but I was fascinated and I asked him if he could show me how to use the bench press and the other weights he had lying around his garage. He kindly agreed and wrote me a program to work different parts of my body on alternate days with rest days in between with all this jargon about sets and reps.

EARLY LESSONS
I enjoyed the feeling of training, it made me feel alive, strong and for the first time in my life I became aware that I could change things in my life using willpower and determination. I had a sense that I was in control. I was changing my physical body; my body was talking to me through the pain in my muscles after a day's training. I learnt that I had to take it slowly, and warm up, and to be patient and that nothing happens instantaneously, just like life. It takes time to build muscles naturally, you can't build muscles overnight.

ANABOLIC STEROIDS
They don't come in a bottle at the supermarket, but anabolic steroids are rampant on the black market. People use these drugs to get results much quicker than by doing it naturally. However, the side effects definitely outweigh the positives and I am totally against anybody using these, as they are destructive to your body.

Some of the side effects include acne, testicular atrophy, paranoia, psychotic rage (also known as 'roid rage'), impotence, enlarged prostate, man boobs, hair loss, high blood pressure, bloating, skin can turn pink in colour, kidney damage and low sperm count.

Once users see the results, they get addicted, want more and start using all different types of steroids to counteract the side effects of the steroids they're taking. They become drug users, and to me, I have never understood why they were doing it because it defeats the purpose of being healthy and looking natural and great. The people that use these in my opinion, don't last long because they're looking for quick gains in a very short time and like to cut corners, and always give up. It's a shame, because I believe they are all good enough to train naturally, eat well and get long lasting results, the way that it should be done.

I've been training for 23 years and have always believed in hard work. To anyone who is thinking about taking anabolic steroids, I would think long and hard before you put that rubbish into your amazing gift that you have been given, because it's your temple. Treat it right and it will happily work wonders for you.

DISCIPLINE FROM TRAINING

Training taught me discipline to follow my program, it made me understand if you want something in life you have to work at it and don't give up, to work smarter not harder, to write down goals that I wanted to achieve and persist with a plan of action. Lifting weights taught me to listen to my body, to tune into the signals and messages it was sending me through pain and muscle soreness.

FEELING GREAT AFTER EXERCISE

After a training session I always felt energised and clear headed. My energy body became lighter, so my frequency was vibrating at a higher rate. My pent up energy had been released and my mental and emotional state had been cleared of any energy blockages. This is when I had such a connection to the universe around me, I had let go of all of life's attachments. I felt as one with everything and everyone. My heaviness had been lifted and I no longer felt handicapped by any insensitivities. I was plugged into the source and it became for me, a natural high. I suggest you try physical activity and feel the benefits for yourself.

BODY STRENGTHENING

I never got sick after I started my training regime, as I later found out, your metabolic rate increases and acts like a natural furnace which cleanses your immune system of any foreign anti-bodies and strengthens it in the process. That's why I still today never get sick of training, and I love to look after my temple, it really is the best health policy.

LESSONS LEARNT THROUGH TRAINING

Training on my temple through exercise taught me about perseverance and stick-ability. That is, if you want to achieve well in life, you can't give up even when the going gets tough, you must plough through to achieve your goals and dreams. It's the person who doesn't quit and believes in themselves in life who will achieve greatly.

The injuries came and went, but it was my determination, my burning desire that fuelled my excitement to become more active, and get a grip on my life that pushed me forward giving me a zest and vitality I had long searched for. I had taken responsibility for myself and I felt great. I thought to myself, if I could do this with my physical body, I could do it with my mental body as well, because they are both connected. A transformation took place. We are all alchemists. If I can do it, so can you!

A NEW SENSE OF WORTH

My observations and feelings just weren't from a physical perspective either. With my new look, I had a new sense of worth. I believed if I could change my physical appearance I could definitely alter my thoughts and perspective in my life as well.

I no longer spoke about myself negatively to anyone. I began to treat myself with respect and dignity. For the first time in my life I was receiving compliments from friends, family and strangers and the opposite sex found me attractive, which I really liked. I was being admired for actively changing my body and my attitude towards myself and others skyrocketed.

My self-esteem was through the roof, and I no longer looked down at the pavement, when I walked, I would walk with my head held high. I felt great about myself, knowing if I could do this, I could do anything. It's amazing what a healthy self-image can do for oneself in the midst of everyday life, and how people in society treat you. We are a reflection of this self-image, in how much we love and respect ourselves.

When I look back on those days and even 23 years later, I'm still looking after my temple, training taught me a lot. I have carried through the same principles which have made me the happy and successful person that I am today. I didn't set out to learn these principles though, it just happened naturally and progressively. This is what looking after myself had taught me.

DEVELOPING FROM THE OUTSIDE IN

I learnt about dedication, commitment, motivation, perseverance, goal setting and sticking to a plan of action, to take responsibility for myself and my life. And if you want to change your life, you must change and work at it, nothing comes for free, don't sit down and play the victim, let go of self-pity and excuses, don't be casual about it otherwise you'll end up being the casualty in your life.

I learnt not to give up and to soldier on, sometimes things in life get tough, but you have to get tougher on yourself and be adaptable, persevere as well as being versatile. While all this was happening, I developed on the inside as well, through my mind power, and found that the rewards were huge. I became more self-confident, I had more self-esteem and self-worth, my values and how I chose to see people and life in general was of a positive attitude and a feeling of good will to all. I became at peace with myself and I no longer was critical of myself or others which made me a happier person to be around. I became a reflection of what I wanted to see in my life and I liked what I saw. I had taken control of my life and it felt great to be in the driver's seat.

> If you have built castles in the air, your work need not be lost; that is where they should be. Now put the foundations under them.
> – HENRY DAVID THOREAU

BODY MIND CONNECTION

At this very moment, I learnt that the body and mind are connected and you must be in balance on the inside as well as the outside. What comes from inside you reflects your outside appearance and reality. If you're busy on the inside mentally, you're going to be trapped physically on the outside, and your outside appearance will reaffirm this fact.

Chris, if you're reading this book, thank-you for introducing me to exercise and all its benefits. And for all those people reading this, take note, you can start an exercise plan, I know it will work wonders for you, as it has done for me.

BEGIN AN EXERCISE PLAN

It's time to start looking after your body. Begin an exercise plan to change your self-image. This will uplift your energy and vitality and kick start a new way of living before its too late. Let's start now! Don't you think it's time to get into shape?

When you change your physical appearance, you'll change mentally and emotionally as well. It's a natural law. What is within will also be reflected on the outside. This is the law of cause and effect.

What will it take for you to start looking after yourself? The doctor telling you you're a prime candidate for a stroke or heart attack because your blood pressure is too high and you could go into cardiac arrest at any moment? Do you want to be around for your children to grow up and see their children? Or, just to do the everyday activities we take for granted, like taking the kids to the park, walking the dog, or going for a swim at the beach? You can do this and much more. Are you ready?

TAKE RESPONSIBILITY FOR YOUR HEALTH

Don't become a victim or another statistic; it's time to take responsibility for your health and your body. It's time to stop taking your body for granted, stop mistreating it and let go of any resentment you have towards your body, work with it and not against it. Stop overloading it with tobacco, drugs, saturated fats, refined sugars, pre-packaged meals loaded with food flavourings, colouring, additives and preservatives. This also applies to carbonated drinks and artificial sweeteners. These can all be harmful to your body and mind.

No wonder there is a growing trend of obesity in first world countries, we are living in affluent times. Children are affected as well, they can be overweight for their age and height, and have more food allergies than ever before.

Remember, you are what you eat, literally. Follow the eating patterns our ancestors did, only fresh and sustainable food consumed as a fuel source for your body, and you will notice a remarkable difference to how you feel.

IT'S A MATTER OF PRIORITIES

We need to get our priorities right. Our body is our temple, it's the best gift we have been given; we must look after it and maintain it to get the best performance out of it. Our body is our best friend so treat it with the respect it deserves. We only get one; it's your vehicle to get around in while you're here in this physical dimension. While we're alive we must treat it with love and respect and it will be loyal to us just like any good friend.

Your material possessions and everything you wish to obtain will be no good to you if you don't have your health. Once your health is gone and your body has deteriorated due to improper care, you will wish you had another chance to look after it. Sometimes we don't get second chances.

Love it, treat it right, respect it and the rewards will be a long and happy, healthy life and you can enjoy all of your possessions knowing you did it through a balance of work, play, exercise and the right nutrition and mental outlook.

LOVE WHO YOU ARE

While you're in your own home, I want you to go to the mirror and take off your clothes and admire your body. What do you find attractive about your body, what don't you like? What parts of your body would you like to change? This exercise is to give you an awareness of your body; this is what you look like for now, however you can change certain physical aspects if you're willing and determined to make the change.

Understand you can't change your height, well I guess you can if you want to take things to an extreme for a few extra centimetres, but bone structure and build are completely genetic. So, some things you have to accept and that's ok.

There are no perfect people out there, even all those so called beautiful people that get displayed on billboards, television, magazines and the movies all have flaws like you and me. It's amazing what make-up and some clever lighting and photo editing can do.

It's just that as people we have been programmed and conditioned by all forms of media and culture, that a certain look is more attractive than another. All this does is segregates people, puts people into certain boxes which makes people feel insecure and inferior to how they should look and behave, and measure up to.

We are all from the same source. It's all an illusion. Don't believe the hype. There are a lot of underweight and thin people out there who aren't healthy just as there are people who are rounded, voluptuous and healthy.

It's disappointing to note that most Australian women think they are larger than they actually are; 45 percent of women and 23 percent of men in the healthy weight range think they are overweight. Love yourself, your uniqueness, there is no-one else like you in the world, embrace your individuality. Let go of any cultural programming and detach yourself from the web of the ego and be free from the strings which keep you bound into superficiality as we are all part of the same whole. Let's get substance back into your life.

> In so much as love grows in you, in so much beauty grows;
> for love is itself the beauty of the soul.
> – ST AUGUSTINE

EXERCISE COMES IN MANY FORMS

Now, you don't have to be like me and exercise in the gym for 45 minutes a day, four times a week for the next 23 years. Make sure you change your routine from time to time to keep things fresh and interesting. We're all different, we come in all different shapes and sizes. Exercise comes in many forms all you have to do is make a conscious decision to begin and find an exercise routine that suits you.

It can be walking, dancing, swimming, playing a particular sport that keeps you interested and involved. Start off slowly, and don't get discouraged, keep going until it becomes a good habit and a routine. It's better to do something than nothing at all. Enjoy the activity for what it is, exercise.

Build momentum each day and don't give up. If you get sore have a rest, then start again, listen to your body and the messages it sends. If you get bored or need some help keeping motivated, get a training partner, join a group, connect with a friend, or join a team sport which can be great for support and motivation.

GET TO KNOW YOUR BODY

When I started training, I was no Arnold Schwarzenegger, but I didn't want to be either. I just worked with what my body could handle until I improved and progressed. I stuck within my limits and worked on improving myself.

Enjoy and get to know your body, it will surprise you by what it can do and what you're capable of. I would remind myself that Rome wasn't built in a day, but I knew that in time it was built, and this helped with my motivation and perseverance not to give up. I knew that I would get there. I enjoyed learning about myself while training.

Progress takes time, but the rewards are well worth it. You become stronger and flexible; get muscle tone, the heart and lungs become stronger and your cardiovascular fitness increases while your blood pressure decreases. These are just the physical aspects of training, additional benefits include feeling great emotionally and mentally.

MAINTAIN MODERATION

Bone density becomes stronger when you exercise, so it's a great health insurance policy for when you're in your twilight years.

Exercise is also great for clearing blocked emotional energies as well as stimulating your nervous system. You will always feel great after exercise as you release natural endorphins from your pituitary gland that lift your mood and make you feel great.

Remember, there must be a balance in everything and you shouldn't overdo it, because then it turns into an addiction, which is an escape from reality and that's not the reason you started exercising in the first place.

Everything in moderation; always listen to yourself because your body will talk to you through your intuition and through the way you feel. If you feel tired or sore, have a day or two off. Listen and work within your body's physical limits.

HEALTHY EATING

With your new healthy attitude towards your body you won't want to eat toxic foods anymore. It defeats the purpose if you're training hard and exercising correctly. By eating the correct foods, the healthiest option will get the best results in the shortest amount of time. Change the portion sizes on your plate, eat smaller meals more often to speed up your metabolism. Generally speaking, we may take in toxic foods that don't agree with us, and we may eat too fast and eat too much. To make sure you're eating the right foods, a good start would be to have an allergy test from a certified doctor or naturopath. This test will let you know what foods and preservatives stress your body's immune system and make you unwell through allergic reactions.

EAT RIGHT FOR YOUR TYPE

Another way to make sure you're eating right for your body in its biological composition is to read the book by Dr Peter D'Adam called *Eat Right for Your Type*. D'Adam is a naturopath and doctor who believes that your blood type determines your susceptibility to certain illnesses. The book covers foods that are excellent for certain blood types and that won't affect the digestive system and how some other foods are bad for a blood type and may be good for another. It's an interesting read which may be of benefit to you as it was for me.

MONITOR FOOD INTAKE

By not overloading your body with copious amounts of food you will feel a lot lighter, your vibration will be a lot faster so you won't feel so heavy and lethargic. Have you ever felt really bloated and heavy after eating too much, or eating foods that don't agree with you and make you feel miserable and depressed? Okay, so you know how this feels, this is the opposite of what we want to achieve. Monitor your food intake and those certain foods that don't agree with you. It's time to get off the merry go round and put your health first.

Start to eat frequently, smaller meals every couple of hours with the right amount of food, and better quality food, fresh fruit and vegetables and lean meats and fish will make you feel better, increase your concentration, reduce headaches and feelings of lethargy. Eating this way also speeds up your metabolism so your fire is stoked all the time, which will stop you from grabbing snacks and picking foods which don't have any nutritional value and therefore make you put on weight.

I made an observation that to get the best out of my body, I had to put the right fuel into it. A Ferrari doesn't run on regular unleaded, it has to run on the highest octane unleaded there is to get the most out of the engine and run at its ultimate potential. We need to eat the right foods for our bodies so we can operate and function correctly every day so we don't get sick and suffer mental and physical breakdown.

AVOID REFINED AND PROCESSED FOODS

Have you ever noticed how you feel after eating refined and processed foods high in saturated fats, washed down with alcohol or carbonated sugar-loaded drinks? You may feel great while you're eating or drinking it, but after you've finished, your energy levels and your mental outlook will be very low. That's your body struggling to derive any goodness from the inferior foods and drinks you're supplying it with as they are superficial and artificial. There is nothing nutritious in sugars and foods containing empty calories. Only supply your body with the best fuel. What you put in is what you get out.

Don't you think it's about time you started to take care of your body on the inside — your (positive) mental outlook, and the outside — by exercising, feeding it the right nutrition at the right times? You can look and feel great, which in turn will give you a positive attitude and a healthy outlook on life and your place in it. I believe you're worth it.

> If we don't take good care of our body, where will we live?
> — ANONYMOUS

ACHIEVE BALANCE

To live a happy fulfilled life you must achieve a balance between your mind and body. Love the way you look, be happy in your own skin and express your thoughts and feelings, so no trapped energies can become blocked and keep you feeling down about your life. Remember, all physical ailments stem from mental and emotional imbalances so it's wise to let out how you're feeling before you become physically ill.

When your body and mind are in good partnership together and are resonating at the same frequency, you will always be happy and positive about life. You'll have the ability to listen to your intuition and follow your heart and your body will always work at its full potential without any aches and pains because you will feel connected to the universe and those around you.

Looking after your temple will be the best investment you can do for yourself. Remember you only get one. It's time you started taking the appropriate action so you can be stronger, healthier, happier and free from aches and pains, so you can enjoy your life and its many wonders.

It's important you understand the mind and the body are connected. The two must work together in unison so you can live life to your full potential. Stay focused, exercise, don't give up, give your body the right nourishment, don't take it for granted, love it and treat it with the respect it deserves. I know you're up for the challenge. What have you got to lose? Only your health…Or your life!

The human body is the best picture of the human soul.
– LUDWIG WITTGENSTEIN

TWELVE
Money...it's just energy

> If money is your hope for independence you will never have it. The only real security that a man will have in this world is a reserve of knowledge, experience and ability.
> — HENRY FORD

I hope by now that you've come to the conclusion that thoughts and beliefs determine a lot in our lives. The way we feel inside determines what we receive on the outside. All wealth begins in the mind. By understanding this you'll start to live abundantly in all areas of your life. You create your life by your attitude and what you believe you deserve. If you want the best no-one is saying you can't have it, nine times out of ten we're the ones that stop ourselves from achieving a fulfilled life.

WHAT MONEY SIGNALS ARE YOU SENDING OUT?

Money is energy and depending on the types of signals you're sending out into the energy web, you're either going to have a good or bad relationship with it.

If you have a bad relationship with money your belief system will be along the lines of some of these sayings, "Money is no good", "I never have enough money", "Money is the root of all evil", "I'm always broke" and my favourite destructive belief of all time is, "Money doesn't grow on trees". If you believe any of these it's no wonder your relationship with money is poor. You can't go giving the energy matrix mixed signals.

Consciously, you want more money, but subconsciously you have a negative attitude towards it and the ways you're going about to obtain it, because your conscious and subconscious mind aren't congruent to what you want. So, these signals are getting repelled, because they aren't on the same wavelength to what you want to attract. Therefore, the universe doesn't provide.

Life will always give you what you expect, nothing more, nothing less, it's the law of attraction. Remember this expression, "Wherever attention flows, energy goes" or "What you focus on, it expands". Well it works with money as well...it's only energy.

MONEY AFFIRMATIONS

If your relationship with money is a good one, your beliefs and your attitude and the way you act towards it will be a positive one. Your thoughts should sound something like this, "I always have lots of money", "Money comes easily", "Money just flows into my life", "There's more than enough money to go round", "I like to share the wealth", and "Money comes to me when I least expect it". This is having an attitude of abundance and having a prosperity consciousness.

There are no mixed signals here if you act in accordance with what you believe. Life will give you what you want, it's that simple. It's a no brainer, your consciousness — it's your energy — let it work for you. Start acting wealthy and you become wealthy. If you want to be poor and live on Struggle Street, act poor. Your actions and your beliefs must be on the same level and let this formula work for you, give it a try.

> To you the earth yields her fruit, and you shall
> not want if you know how to fill your hands.
> — KHALIL GIBRAN

ABANDON DYSFUNCTIONAL BELIEFS

I want to get rid of some old dysfunctional belief patterns about money and how you can obtain freedom and become more prosperous and have abundance in your life.

It's not your job or how much money you make, it's your attitude and your belief system towards the job that will make the difference. When I was putting myself through college and working part-time in the local petrol station I actually really enjoyed it. Not once did I get depressed, I was too busy enjoying myself being in the moment, and playing my role as a petrol station attendant. I was meeting various types of people from all walks of life, making contacts, developing my communication skills and enjoying the fast pace and diversity of it all. In fact, I was grateful to have a job, so I could pay for my college fees, and have some spare time after work to develop my own business and get myself ready for a prosperous future.

I can remember the other casual staff always complaining about never having enough money to live on, and all their worries that came with it. They would say things such as, "I can't pay for my bills and petrol prices are going through the roof." All I could think to myself was we're all getting paid the same so why are they acting like this when we're all in the same boat?

IT'S YOUR ATTITUDE

It came to me in an instant that it's your attitude, your positive beliefs and a plan of action which will work for your best interests that makes all the difference between the haves and have-nots.

Some of the staff never had enough money left over until pay day and were always broke, while I always had enough money to put into my savings account to put myself through college. I was doing more with my money and putting it towards a higher education and protecting my home court advantage (looking after myself). It's about what your priorities are and where you invest your time and money.

Remember this, it's not what's happening out in the physical world that affects you, it's what is going on in your inside world. So, your attitude, your actions and making money vibrate to you with your thoughts and your programs that run either positively or negatively in your subconscious mind, will have the ultimate say on what you have and how you live your life, abundantly or not.

INSTANT MILLIONAIRES

Take, for instance, those feel good stories you hear on the radio, where people have been unemployed or living on the poverty line and then become instant millionaires in the lottery. Unfortunately, that's where the fairytale usually ends. These people generally don't have prosperity consciousness and believe they are not worthy of having such wealth. They feel uncomfortable with their mass winnings and usually become worse off, because their belief system, actions and attitudes haven't changed when winning the money. They didn't change their beliefs to a much more positive vibration of abundance. Life will produce many circumstances and scenarios for them to part ways with it. By not thinking abundantly and having a new prosperity consciousness, a person will always find ways to part with their money.

YOU DESERVE IT

Believe that you're worthy of having money, obtaining and keeping it, and there's an abundance of money to go around. You're just as special as anybody else, you deserve it as well.

Please don't be a tight wad and try and hold onto every cent that you earn. If you're doing this, it's dysfunctional behaviour, stop this now. What you're doing is sending out signals to the energy web, that money is really hard to come by and it's scarce in your life so you hold onto every last cent. I know people like this. It's funny in a weird way. They will say things such as "I forgot my wallet!", or "I'll pay you back". Ever heard these? Nice ones.

You must detach yourself from money and act like you've got lots of it coming to you, in numerous amounts. This is how the wealthy act, they don't act desperate and put up mental blocks which stop the flow of money coming to them. They let it flow to them, they don't chase it.

Start trusting yourself with money, carry more, so it will make you feel prosperous and you act more worthy of receiving it when you get it. This is when you're reprogramming your subconscious mind and your attitudes towards money will become more positive and fruitful.

TAKE ACTION

Below are some strategies and thoughts to help you take charge of your prosperity counsciousness.

- Write up an action plan to use your creativity and ingenuity to make more money. By working on your strengths, talents and abilities and bringing them to the market place you'll make more money as well as enjoy what you do. It's a win-win.
- Examples include making clothes or accessories that you often get complimented on, or even baby clothes. Start your own fashion label and take your products to the markets on weekends to get your name out there.
- Harness your talents such as photography or writing. It could be the impetus you need to get started to write your own book, or sell your photographs or photography services. Not only will you enjoy what you do, but you will be making money from it at the same time.
- Have great philosophy on life and money. Your attitude will attract attention to those you want in your life.
- Remember, money is a by-product for goods and services

rendered. Money doesn't make you rich. It's your talents, abilities and services that are sought after in the market place. So, love what you do, be the best at what you do, stand out, give better service, don't undercut your products or services to get more sales or clients, because you're going to have to work harder not smarter. Believe in yourself and what you have to offer. This is the key.
- Read up on financial books. Whether you want to budget more effectively or learn about investments in real estate, the stock market, or a self-managed superannuation fund — knowledge is imperative.
- Have more than one skill. The more skills you have, the more employable and valuable you are to your employer and the market place.
- Be bi-lingual. The more languages you speak, the better the job and travel opportunities you'll have to explore the world.

> Do not hire a man who does your work for money, but him who does it for the love of it.
> – HENRY DAVID THOREAU

INVEST YOUR MONEY

Below are some simple tips and strategies to get you thinking about investing your money for the future.

- Spend less than you earn, save and invest the difference for your future.
- Work out a budget of your expenses and your current income to identify where you may be able to make savings.
- Develop a short-term plan (goals could include starting a savings plan, learning better budgeting skills, or cutting expenses so your family can take a holiday).
- Create a mid-term plan (once you've established your goals work out how and when you can achieve them). Once you have learnt some good savings habits and routines, set up a fixed term deposit or high interest account to make your savings work for you.
- Work out a long-term plan (goals could include a long-term growth portfolio, or paying off the mortgage sooner.)

- Let your money work for you while you're sleeping. You can do this by buying shares, bonds or investing in the stock market or real estate — whatever floats your boat.
- See a financial advisor for investment advice. They can be extremely knowledgeable as long as you find the right one that you feel comfortable with, and who shares your money philosophy.

LOOK PROSPEROUS

Wear nice clothes (they don't need to be expensive or even new) and dress the part. Maintain your appearance and self-image and hold your head up high. Watch how people treat you and the way you feel about yourself, more importantly. Your confidence and self-worth will go through the roof as you're vibrating the frequency of abundance, and prosperity will be oozing out of your pores.

Understand when you become comfortable with who you are, you magnetise what you want around you. People, chance meetings and opportunities will come knocking at your door. When you become more enthusiastic about who you are, watch your motivation and positive beliefs lift your spirits up and your ambition and life will pull you where you need to be, in the now. The law of attraction will be at work here. What you put out is what you get back, have faith and trust it.

If you know any successful people become more acquainted with them. Ask them for guidance or better still ask them to be a mentor, it'll boost their ego and give you strategies and innovative ways to boost your bank balance and show what money can do for you in a positive way. Become in harmony and resonate with these successful people. The results will amaze you. Success is very catchy especially when you're surrounded by its many influences and are in the right environment.

> One that desires to excel should endeavour in those things that are in themselves most excellent.
> – EPICTETUS

FAKE IT UNTIL YOU MAKE IT

Fake it until you make it, remember your subconscious mind can't tell the difference between what is real or not. So live it, feel it, affirm it, visualise it, embrace it and most importantly, believe it. When you become prosperous you know it was only a matter of time and your hard work has paid off. Open up the channels of money consciousness, let the energy flow into your life, don't attach or grasp but let the money flow to you.

Life will only give you what you expect and feel like you deserve. So believe, have positive thoughts, make financial plans, put the effort in and become responsible for your life and take the initiative today to make money attract to you, like moths to a naked flame. Because in the end, it's just energy.

> Money is usually attracted, not pursued.
> — JIM ROHN

THIRTEEN
It's time for a spring clean... in your life

> I often think you bring unhappiness on yourself, because if you don't like yourself very much, you allow yourself to be influenced by people who reinforce that.
> — LYNN JOHNSTON

When was the last time you gave your home a good cleaning out? A good cleaning out involves getting rid of all the dust and grime, removing rubbish and items hoarded away. What about your car, when was the last time you took the time to vacuum inside the car? Including washing the exterior, cleaning the wheels, checking the oil and all engine components to make sure it's working well and in good driving order?

When you finally get enough enthusiasm and effort to cleanse and detoxify your private spaces, you make the energy flow better and create an environment that uplifts your spirits. It will make you feel better about yourself, calmer, relaxed and in a much clearer head space.

DECLUTTER YOUR ENVIRONMENT

Appreciating what you have in your life and the environment that you surround yourself in can have a major influence on the choices you make.

Have you ever gone into a friend's home or car and it was untidy, smelly and just generally not clean? How did this environment make you feel? Uncomfortable, disgusted, ill, or perhaps you just wanted to get out of there? Or was the space clean, lovely and organised with a positive energy which made you comfortable and relaxed?

This is how our environment influences the decisions we make from day to day. If your environment is clean and tidy and the energy is free flowing, you'll be in a good head space to make the right decisions. If it's messy and in disarray your mind will be all over the place, just like the environment you surround yourself in.

The same can be said about our lives and even the friendships we develop. What and who you surround yourself with can be good or can be detrimental to us on an energetic, mental, emotional and spiritual level.

What do you think about people who live in cluttered environments, do you think their minds are clear, focussed and they can concentrate easily? Or would you presume their minds are racy and their thoughts and actions are scattered? It may make you think they are less in control of their lives. Pay close attention to the people you know and you'll get a sense of their environments and its impact on their mind and thought patterns. It's very interesting.

Every day we are influenced by our immediate environment as well as our extended environment in our community and society. We can mostly control our immediate environment which includes family, friends, work and home life. The impact of the wider environment in our lives is harder to control. We are constantly bombarded by the mass media through television, radio and magazines, and even social media. However, we can control who we choose to let into our lives. It's time to filter out the garbage.

> An insincere and evil friend is more to be feared than a wild beast, a wild beast may wound your body, but an evil friend will wound your mind.
> – BUDDHA

BE SELECTIVE WITH FRIENDS

You must take control and filter out what you want in and out of your life to give you the best possible chance of living the life you want. Because if you don't, the people and other certain influences will make an outstanding difference to the way you think, the way you feel and in turn your actions and generally how you live your life.

Be careful of being caught out with friends, sometimes they wear different masks because they have different agendas to what their smiling face makes you want to believe. They want to make you happy and can't do enough for you but if they don't get what they want, there can be repercussions.

Or, sometimes there are people you know who you only hear from when they want something. You know who they are, I call them parasites, they feed off the host leaving you drained and when they've got what they want they leave. We all know so called friends like this, don't we? I use the term friends very lightly. It's time to get out the insecticide and weed these so called friends out of your life. I have, and I feel much better for it — physically, mentally and energetically.

It's not only the fake and dishonest friends you have to be careful of. Some are loving and caring to your face, then do a back-flip because they become jealous, envious, abuse your trust, or spread rumours and lies to defame your character or put you down. These people are poison to your soul.

They can be described as leeches because they're negative, they hold you back and down, and suck the life force out of you. They are dangerous to your wellbeing. What are they bringing to the table to make you feel better about yourself and bring out your finer points? If you hang around them you better be careful otherwise you'll morph into one of them! Oh no — look out! There's an old saying, "Birds of a feather, flock together" it's time for a spring clean! It's your life, your choice. I've seen beautiful people turn into devils really quickly because of the company they kept, have you?

To weed these people out of your life, you must listen to your intuition and act on it. If you want to have good friends in your life you have to be a good reader of people and listen to how you feel in their presence. A true friend will accept you as you are, encourage you, nuture you, and be there when you need them most.

> The key is to keep company only with people who uplift you, whose presence calls forth your best.
> – EPICTETUS

ATTRACT POSITIVE FRIENDS

You can tell a lot about a person by the company they keep. If you really want to get to know someone you only have to see who their friends are. Their friends will tell you what values, morals, how much integrity they have as well as how they see themselves. Are they worthy of love and respect or do they treat others with no respect or common courtesy?

If you want good friends they must be honest with you, loyal, reliable, and trustworthy. Having a close circle of friends can be a great influence on you. They can pick you up when you're down; give you courage and motivation when you're wavering and undecided in your time of need.

I like to have friends I can learn from because I like to be mentally stimulated. They keep me on my toes in the knowledge department. I've been really blessed with good friends my whole life, they have all been my teachers and I thank them for that. I believe I have a part of all my friends' character traits in me, that's why I get along with them, we all vibrate at the same frequency so we attract one another into each others' lives.

> A man's growth is seen in the successive choirs of his friends.
> — RALPH WALDO EMERSON

THE BUTTERFLIES

Now, let's look at the positive people in your life, you know the ones who make you laugh and smile, that encourage you to do your best. They are there when you need them. These people are always doing their best for you and others, looking for new opportunities all the time, are focused and goal oriented.

These people are called 'butterflies', they're forever on the ball, doing things that excite them and inspire you to do better with yourself and your life. They have always got something on the go and have an abundance of energy and a zest for life. I love these people. I suggest you welcome more 'butterflies' into your life surround yourself with people like this. They will believe in you and encourage you to live up to your full potential, because they will tell you you're worth it. They will lift you up with their beautiful wings and let you soar where others won't tread. These people are angels in disguise.

MAKE THE DECISION

You have a decision to make here. Do you want to surround yourself with people who are lazy, critical, rude, judgemental, and draining, or people who are happy, friendly, spontaneous, driven, focused, positive and successful? Set the bar high with friends and those that you allow into your life. Don't become mundane, boring or comfortable there is no growth or change in being complacent, just more of the same, day in and day out.

You are affected by your environment and the people you surround yourself with, so choose wisely.

> Before we make friends with anyone else,
> we must first make friends with ourselves.
> – ELEANOR ROOSEVELT

IT'S UP TO YOU

I believe you have a choice of action, an ability to choose your attitudes towards the environmental factors you find yourself surrounded in. Whether they be psychological, sociological or biological.

It's our right as spiritual beings having an earthly experience to overcome any challenges put in our way. By the way you think, positive or negative, you have a choice to be a product of your surroundings, to be moulded by circumstance. Or you can choose your own way, believing in yourself and holding steadfast and not becoming a product of the people and the environment you find yourself in. It's your decision.

By becoming active and giving yourself a purpose to strive for, you will obtain opportunity and fulfilment of the highest nature. You must know, you are worthy of succeeding in your life. You must stay true to yourself and not be influenced by other people's opinions and by what they say. Napoleon Hill once said, "Whatever the mind can conceive and believe, the mind can achieve." I couldn't say it better myself. As Friedrich Nietzsche said, "He who has a why to live for can bear almost any how."

When you let go of the stagnant energy in your life, you create space for new and wonderful things to come into that space. Friendlier people, new relationships, greater job prospects. Your mental outlook will be more positive and new thoughts and ideas will lead you down a new and exciting path.

This is your life, it's time for a spring clean, make the all important decision to detoxify and love yourself and know who you are. Oh, one last thing, are you a leech or a butterfly?

> What you bring forth out of yourself from the inside will save you. What you do not bring forth out of yourself from the inside will destroy you.
> – GOSPEL OF THOMAS

FOURTEEN

What mask are you wearing today?

> It is very necessary that a man should be appraised early in life, that it is a masquerade in which he finds himself, for otherwise, there are many things which he will fail to understand.
> – ARTHUR SCHOPENHAUER

Throughout my life I have noticed and observed that as people in society we wear many masks throughout the stages of our development and growth, to fit in with others. In daily life the majority of people conform to the expectations of loved ones, friends, work colleagues and strangers. We do this so as not to offend them and not to be seen as different, or unusual in our actions or behaviour, and generally to conform to society.

There is this unseen force which holds us and suppresses us not to step on someone else's toes, to do the right thing, not to speak the truth, or so we don't make a fool of ourselves or hurt someone else's feelings. But what about your feelings and your true self, your identity, your individuality, where does that retreat to? I know where, in the closet. The majority of people are like turtles, they go into their shell which is their true hidden self, and hide from themselves and others. But you're hurting yourself in the end, for not being genuine and authentic.

LET GO OF THE FAÇADE

It's time to let go of this façade, of what will people think of you. Cut the imaginary chains that keep you bound from your true self. I want you to embrace your uniqueness, be truly open to all experiences, listen to your heart, follow your path and stop deceiving yourself.

When you're being authentic in your life and you're expressing truth to yourself and the world around you, your fifth chakra will be open and free of any imbalances of consciousness (energy). As covered in chapter one, the fifth chakra is located in the throat area. By having the willpower to express freely who you are by saying what you need to say and speaking truthfully, you're not wearing any masks, but only being your true self. When you do this you have taken responsibility to make choices in your life that suit what you want and what you represent, not what you should do or what's expected of you.

This will allow you to fulfil your inner most dreams and live according to who you are and not have to play a certain role that makes you physically sick and emotionally and mentally unhappy. If you're not in control of yourself and express who you are in your own unique and creative way, you're living with many masks and you become a stranger to yourself and those that love you.

It's time for you to listen to your heart and let your mind communicate with your heart. Be your own truth, and the neck stiffness, headaches and the sore throats will disappear. If you're head and heart aren't working together in your life, guess what's caught in the middle? Your neck, which is where your fifth chakra is located, you guessed it!

If you're not happy, speak your mind, be free, let go of all expectations that people place upon you. Let others around you enjoy their lies and deceptions and the games that they play. It's time to really live your life and let go of all the small and closed minded people who try and disempower you.

"I AM ME, AND I AM FREE"

Today is a new day, time for new beginnings, a new page, one door shuts and another opens. It's time to come out into the open and announce, "I am me and I am free". Right now, I want you to go to that place where you hide and throw away all of your masks. Keep only one, the authentic one. Wear your real mask, the one that you should be proud to wear, with no hang-ups as to what other people say or think about you. Be true, love yourself, be yourself.

> Is freedom anything else than the right to live as we wish? Nothing else.
> – EPICTETUS

If you want to be happy and truly fulfilled in your life you have to love yourself right now, you're perfect and beautiful in every way. Enjoy your journey, because you're special, we all are. Let go of the ego which keeps you separate from everything and everyone, no more labels, no two people are the same in this life. Let go of all the falsities that you hide behind, because at this moment you're no longer a pawn for society's hang-ups and complexities.

It's time to let your true self shine, embrace your identity, your emotions and feelings because they are real and honest. Don't inhibit yourself, you're better than that, speak your mind, be heard, your inner will is in your hands, express yourself and stand your ground, be an unshakeable force.

When you start living your life for who you really are, true inner fulfilment and happiness will be yours. Your spirit will rejoice because the charade will be over.

I want you to enjoy your transformations, let the building process begin in your life. Make mistakes, learn from them, grow and mature, this is how we evolve as human beings. You will sail unchartered waters, but enjoy the experience, these will be magical moments for you, something to remember and reflect on. Don't go back, press on.

> Ships in harbour are safe, but that's not what ships are built for.
> – JOHN A. SHEDD

Your confidence, self-esteem and self-worth will be at heights you have never experienced before and exhilaration will be yours. You'll be more open, frank and trusting, because people can either take you or leave you.

Let people be themselves, without judgement or criticism, people will love you for being real. And, in return your interactions with people will become meaningful and genuine.

As all of this is happening, your frequency and vibration of your energy body will resonate at higher speeds making you lose contact of all your fickle and superficial friends. No loss there! They will continue to wear many masks, depending on their agenda and what role they're playing, they won't be able to handle the new you. It will be uncomfortable for them to be in your presence, as their energy vibration is of a lower frequency. They haven't changed and you have, so you won't be on the same wavelength any longer, they will repel you and keep away. They'll say things like, "I just don't get you anymore," or "You're just not the same person I once knew."

> Give me beauty in the inward soul;
> may the outward and the inward man be at one.
> — SOCRATES

GOSSIPS

Have you been a victim of someone who has spread rumours and vicious gossip? Or someone who set out to harm you through innuendo? People who gossip or spread rumours like this influence other people who can't think for themselves. They don't ask where the rumours are coming from; and they don't ask what is the source or the motives behind the people who do such acts?

I have learnt that people believe what they hear, not what they experience or see for themselves. Their minds are closed, they have blinkers on and quite often just don't care whose lives or feelings they are affecting.

We have been programmed and conditioned to take information as gospel when we should ask questions and seek the truth for ourselves. There are always two sides to a story. The way you treat yourself is reflective on how you treat others. When you have an open mind and an open heart, your thoughts will not be affected by your negative mindset or environment.

> I care not so much what I am in the opinion of others, as what I am in my own; I would be rich of myself, and not by borrowing.
> — MICHEL DE MONTAIGNE

One last thing I want to share with my teachers, those of you who have worn false masks — you have taught me valuable lessons and tempered me to be the man I am today, just like a fine Samurai sword, for that I can say thank you! I have found in the end people always show their true colours.

> Hardly one in ten thousand will have the strength of mind to ask himself seriously and earnestly, "Is that true?"
> — ARTHUR SCHOPENHAUER

The majority of people tend to believe what they hear and have been told, without real evidence to support their beliefs. It's time to ask questions, just as this story suggests.

Discover Your Path

A guy is walking down the street one night and passes a man under a street lamp on his hands and knees looking for something. "Lost something?" the man asks. "My car keys," the man replies. "Where did you last see them?" The man points to a dark alleyway down the street. "If you lost them over there why are you searching for them over here?" He said, "Because this is where the light is!" Do you live your life like this? Open up your mind, ask questions and listen to yourself for the answers. To be yourself you must think for yourself.

> Be more concerned with your character than your reputation, because your character is what you really are, while your reputation is merely what others think you are.
> — JOHN WOODEN

Wear only one mask, your authentic one, be genuine, be sincere and most of all be true to yourself. Embrace your uniqueness it's time for you to get real! How many masks do you have now? Hopefully it's just the one!

> We become so accustomed to disguise ourselves to others that at last we are disguised to ourselves.
> — LA ROCHEFOUCAULD

FIFTEEN

It's time to reconnect ...with people

It's not too late to develop new friendships or reconnect with people.
– MORRIE SCHWARTZ

We're living in the most opportunistic of times that the world has ever known. The internet has connected the world and made it so convenient for everyone to live their lives. We can work from home and communicate with anyone around the world at the touch of a button. It doesn't matter what country you're in or on which hemisphere. The internet allows you to buy and sell products and services for practically everything imagineable. You don't even have to go to the supermarket to buy groceries anymore, you can buy online and have it delivered it straight to your door. You can book a hotel on the other side of the world, it is only a few clicks away. Even meeting the love of your life and the person of your dreams can be done online with the many dating sites. Convenience, convenience, convenience, or is it? Hang on, my smart phone is ringing. Sorry, it was just a text message!

DON'T LOSE THE HUMAN CONNECTION

I have witnessed and observed that as people we are losing touch with ourselves and each other. Because of all this technology, we're losing our interpersonal skills to communicate with one another and the emotional intelligence to express ourselves as only human beings can.

Being human is about being connected spiritually, emotionally and mentally with people and being of service to our fellow brothers and sisters, to make life easier for everybody to live here on this beautiful planet. Many people are turning into robots who don't feel love or compassion and treating people like pawns in their selfish games of manipulation. They have greed for everything their hearts' desire and they don't care who they hurt or who they step over to get what they want. Superficiality rules the day, and substance has left the building.

Discover Your Path

> We are all so much together but we are all dying of loneliness.
> – DR ALBERT SCHWEITZER

People are being asked out, or dumped, and even fired from their jobs (hopefully not at the same time) through text messaging.

You go to a restaurant to enjoy dinner and good conversation and people are too busy looking at their tablet computers and ignoring one another as they check emails and messages on their smart phones. It's the same scenario on public transport, no-one talks or engages in conversation anymore, let alone looks at anyone.

Let's all put on our blank face mask! The one that says, "Don't look at me, don't notice me, I don't want to talk to you!" Few people make eye contact anymore. What a cold and lifeless society we have become.

Family relationships are being fractured over many issues including family, relationship or financial issues. Generally speaking, the family unit is not what it once was, some would even say it has broken down; some young families don't even sit down at the dinner table for a meal anymore.

Children have lost respect for their elders and some parents don't have a clue about what their children are getting up to. I've seen three year olds with their own tablet computers.

Young girls are growing up too fast with the clothes they wear (or the lack thereof). Some don't behave like young ladies anymore, they swear, spit and fight and it's all on public display, as if they are proud of their behaviour.

> No tree has branches so foolish as to fight among themselves.
> – NATIVE AMERICAN PROVERB

BACK TO BASICS

Call me old fashioned, but I believe we need to go back to basics with the use of manners, courtesy and decent behaviour. We need to set boundaries on what is acceptable and what is not, for the safety, dignity and morality of our children.

If we as a society keep going the way we are, what do you think the future generations will be like? The younger people out there are our leaders of tomorrow, and will only learn from the people they look up to and the environment they're in. The people they admire and idolise are their major influencers such as celebrities, sportspeople, models and anybody else who is in the public eye and gets put on a pedestal.

POOR INFLUENCERS

Unfortunately, it's the wrong people and environments that are influencing them such as television, internet, the movies, social media and other forms of the media. Young people are influenced by celebrities, entertainers, singers, footballers and models, of which some of them don't care what they say or how their bad behaviour can be perceived by those that look up to them.

Some parents also act poorly, using bad language, not taking an interest in their children's development, or acting in a way which is harmful to their children's learning capabilities. Adults should know better as they are seen as role models to younger people and so should act accordingly and take responsibility for their actions.

BAD BEHAVIOUR

Why is it that children as young as ten are on anti-depressants? Why are young girls wearing provocative clothing, just to fit in and be seen as cool by the 'in crowd', so they don't stand out and become targets of bullying? Why is it that young teenagers and young adults are binge drinking themselves into a stupor every weekend or indulging in drugs and falling foul of risky sexual behaviour? Why is it that people are being bashed to death, stabbed or glassed at clubs, parties or just about anywhere for no reason whatsoever?

According to the World Health Organisation, suicide in general has increased up to 60 percent in the last 45 years around the world, that's one death every 40 seconds. Why is this?

Why are police or ambulance officers being attacked for helping people in need, where is the respect for these people trying to help and uphold the law? There are more people leaving the police service than there are joining, that says a lot.

Why are the elderly locking themselves in their houses in 40 degree celcius heat and perishing inside? They are too scared to go beyond their front doors for fear of being robbed or attacked. What ever happened to looking after your elderly neighbours and checking to see if they're alright?

Discover Your Path

> You shall love your neighbour as yourself.
> – JESUS

When was the last time you smiled at someone on the street or shopping centre and you were totally ignored, or they looked at you like you were from outer space?

Circumstances and tragedies are occurring, even now as I write this chapter. Do you know why? This is where you fit into this.

I know you want better for yourself and the people around you and society in general. Otherwise you wouldn't be reading this book of encouragement to live a happy and rewarding life for yourself and others. We're all in this together.

> Connect With People
> If you want to be happy.....
> For an hour, take a nap
> For a day, go fishing
> For a month, get married
> For a year, get an inheritance
> For a lifetime, help someone.
> – CHINESE PROVERB

RECONNECT WITH YOUR CHILDREN

It's time to reconnect with your children. Start now. If you have your own children, teenagers or young adults, are an aunty or an uncle or even a godparent, get involved in their lives. Tell them you love them and want to support them. Become a part of their lives, show them you're interested, teach and nurture them, it's your role as parents or guardians.

It's your duty and responsibility as their guardians and mentors to watch over and protect them and teach them right from wrong. Lead by example. It takes a village to raise a child — they learn from everyone around them.

DEPRESSION

Understand right now someone you care about is probably down in the dumps and could be experiencing depression. The behaviours I have mentioned earlier are tell-tale signs of depression, mental illness, boredom and feelings of emptiness, lack of purpose and meaning in one's life.

It's time to reconnect…with people

Did you know Australia's suicide rate is now twice the road toll? Many of these suicides may have been prevented if the people close to the victims were able to identify these early signs and give the love, care and empathy they needed when they were alive. It could be as simple as asking, "Are you ok?", "Would you like to talk about it?", "What's on your mind?"

According to the Australian Bureau of Statistics:

- 45% of adult Australians will experience mental illness.
- In 2003, mental disorders were identified as the leading cause of healthy years of life lost due to disability.
- 26% of 16 – 24 year olds experienced a mental disorder in the last 12 months.
- Mental disorders are the leading contributor to the total burden of disease among young Australians.
- 12% of 13 – 17 year olds have reported having thought about suicide.
- Suicide is the main cause of premature death among young people with a mental illness.

Enough is enough. People who act in strange ways which are detrimental to their character are hurting inside. They're hurt, lost, feel alone and empty with no purpose and meaning. It's time to take back responsibility not only for ourselves, but to care for others around us. We're all brothers and sisters, it's time to be love in action we all can make the change for the better. Begin this moment!

INTERPERSONAL SKILLS

It's time to develop your interpersonal skills and use your emotional intelligence with everyone, including your loved ones. Open up and be friendly, speak to your neighbours and help strangers in need, show compassion to your fellow travellers, what if the shoe was on the other foot? As Ghandi said, "We must become the change we want to see".

Be respectful of people's needs and wishes and follow the rules and regulations that the law has put in place to keep us safe and out of harm's way so we can live in a civilised society. Do you want to live in a society where there's peace and harmony and it's safe to walk the street? I know I do. If we all get together to do one great act of kindness in the society we live in, people will respond in kind and your positive actions will have a flow on effect, it's so simple but effective.

> Suppose a neighbour should desire to light a candle at your fire, would it deprive your flame of light, because another profits by it.
> – ROBERT LLOYD

If you know someone who's in trouble, down or upset, you can do your best and take the time to say hello. Telephone them and let them know that you care about them, you're thinking of them, and you're there to help. If you know something's not right, act before it's too late.

> We are all branches on this tree called humanity.
> – WAYNE DYER

Go looking for friends and they're hard to find, become friendlier towards people and you'll find friends everywhere. Helping people and being of service makes you feel good and playing your part in society in which you belong. Even when someone watches you help someone it makes them feel better. It's like a chain reaction as the saying goes, "Pay it forward". We're all in this life together, let's all enjoy it together.

> If each of us sweeps in front of our own steps,
> the whole world will be clean.
> – JOHANN WOLFGANG VON GOETHE

RESTORE THE BALANCE

It's time to reconnect with our inner selves, get in touch with who we really are and restore the balance of human ideals. These include respect for ourselves and others, treating people the way we want to be treated, and love for one another and ourselves. We need to communicate on a deeper level, not being petty or superficial. It's time to bring substance back into your soul, get involved in the lives of your loved ones and turn a stranger into a friend. Feel and express more, appreciate and be grateful for being alive, it's a gift, not a given right.

> Prayer in action is love, love in action is service.
> – MOTHER TERESA

Above all else, appreciate that it's an amazing time to be alive, however don't let technology override who you are, your values and morals.

It's time to reconnect...with people

Don't become a robot, with no heart, cold, without any emotion this is not who we are as a populace. We are love and we come from love, understand you're a miracle, worthy of all the happiness and joy in the world.

To enjoy your life, share your experiences with people, the ones that are all around you. When you look at your greatest moments and experiences that you've had, you will realise they are always shared with people, not the television, the computer, your phone. Get rid of your blank stares and replace it with a smile and a hello. It's time to brush up on your communication skills, join the robots rebellion and re-connect with everyone.

> In society as it is now constituted, all the established rules have so many mechanical duties, while real duty consists in obeying the laws of our own being.
> – *VICTOR CHERBULIEZ*

SIXTEEN

Happiness, it's not out there... it's in here

> The happiness we receive from ourselves is greater than which we obtain from our surroundings.
> – METRODORUS

Happiness, it comes from inside you, true fulfilment. It's how you feel about yourself and how you see yourself. Are you happy in your job, your relationship with yourself and others? Are you content with how you've turned out? Do you love and respect yourself or are you unhappy and feel lost? If you feel like this, what are you doing to become fulfilled? Are you putting in the effort to make an improvement in your life or are you just coasting along the sidelines? It's time you took responsibility for your own happiness and became more fulfilled inside.

> To live we must conquer incessantly;
> we must have the courage to be happy.
> – HENRI FREDERIC AMIEL

DETACH YOURSELF

Let's start by detaching ourselves from all the superficial happiness. Do you know what I mean? I'll tell you. I'll be happy when I have my new car, handbag, dress, home, golf clubs, jewellery, appliances for the kitchen, and it goes on, never ending.

This type of happiness is short term, it comes and goes, and definitely doesn't fill the void to what's lacking inside of you. After a few months, the next materialistic item will show up on your radar, to replace the previous. And on it goes, the superficial merry-go-round, never really arriving at anything real or full of substance.

> It's the spirit that gives life, the flesh counts for nothing.
> – JOHN 6:63

YOUNG PRINCE

I would like to share a story about a young prince and his quest for happiness.

> A young and handsome prince had everything life could offer him. Luxury, beautiful women, wealth, designer clothes, fast cars and adventure all at his finger tips, but he wasn't happy. So he went to his doctor, who prescribed a cure. "Have your servant search your town for the happiest person in it; wear their shirt and you'll be happy". So, the prince sent his helpers to find the happiest person, which they did. However, they were unable to bring back his shirt, as he didn't own one, nor did he have any shoes, as he was poor! Understand true happiness is from the soul and not with external, material objects and conditions.

> Folks are about as happy as they make their minds up to be.
> – ABRAHAM LINCOLN

MATERIAL POSSESSIONS

Understand material objects won't quench your thirst for true happiness, fulfilment or wellbeing. I know of people who go into debt to purchase material items to keep up with the Joneses, to feel like they're getting ahead, or doing better than everybody else.

I know people who wear the latest fashion and accessories, purchase large five bedroom homes with only two people living in them, just to make them feel good about themselves. I also know of people who regularly inject collagen in their lips and cheeks and friends who drive flashy sports cars, however, can't even pay the rent or put food on the table, just to make themselves feel happy, fulfilled and worthy. Guess what? They're deluding themselves, and maybe you are too? Happiness won't be found from the outside driven by material conditions, to think like this is petty.

Material possessions are finite and happiness is infinite. Don't let consumerism take over your life. Step outside of the petty and superficial. Get out of the pursuit of being in competition or in a race with others. A person's material wealth isn't the measure of their real wealth, but finding true meaning, purpose and inner fulfilment will nourish their soul and lead them to a life of service, which is love in action.

HAPPINESS IS IN THE NOW

Happiness is found in the now. It's in being grateful for what you have, not what you don't have. When was the last time you looked around and noticed all the good things in your life? And the people in it? I wake up each morning in a soft bed, and the fact I have a roof over my head to keep away the rain, I go to the toilet in a bathroom, and not in a hole in the ground. When I turn on a tap, I have fresh and clean water available, I don't have to walk 100 kilometres to get it out of a well. I can go to the fridge and have something to eat, food is at an arm's reach.

I could go on, but you get my point, don't you? Be grateful and thankful for what you do have. A lot of people around the world as I write this don't have the basic needs for survival like food, shelter and clean water, even now in the 21st century. Money, greed, and consumerism have taken over, yet millions of people don't know how to read and write and people are still starving or in dire poverty and its closer to home than you may think. It's a wakeup call to put your life into perspective and know you are truly blessed.

> Happiness depends upon ourselves.
> – ARISTOTLE

It's amazing how two people can have or be in a certain situation, but react totally differently from each other and experience happiness or misery. Let's take for instance you have been made redundant from your job after 20 years of service. One person might see this as the end of the world and get depressed and want to act like there's no reason to go on living. Another person may see this as an opportunity to experience new possibilities and enjoy their independence, as well as growth, and a sense of freedom or career change.

At the end of the day, the decision lies with you, one path leads to happiness and discovering new possibilities and the other path to misery, loneliness and depression. That's a hard decision to make. Tragedy or growth? It's surprising how many choose the latter!

Yes, you can say that having a positive attitude makes all the difference towards one's challenges and opportunities given in life. A positive attitude can help you through the hardest of times as well as increase your joy and happiness. A negative attitude can make matters so much worse, exasperating pain and suffering and intensifying guilt and worry, which may lead to depression or even dis-ease of the body.

> There is only one way to happiness, and let this rule be ready both in the morning and during the day and by night: the rule is not to look towards things which are out of the power of our will.
> – EPICTETUS

CHALLENGES AND OBSTACLES

The challenges you encounter in life are not your enemies, but your teachers. They have been put in front of you to test and challenge you. Let the adversity in your life temper you and strengthen your foundations. It is from these circumstances that you'll find out who you really are. Look for the positive in every situation. If you focus only on the negatives in all experiences, you're making them become detrimental to your learning and how you progress in the future. Be much kinder to yourself, and stay positive.

> Stand apart from circumstances and do not
> permit them to influence the mind.
> – ZEN

It's not what happens to you in life; it's how you deal with it by taking responsibility for your reactions to life's challenges. Do you react and get defensive, uptight and stressed or are you going to respond to life and go with what your inner heart tells you to do?

> Empty your mind, be formless, shapeless, like water.
> Now you put water into a cup, it becomes the cup,
> You put water into a bottle, it becomes the bottle,
> You put it into a teapot, it becomes the teapot,
> Water can flow or it can crash!
> Be water my friend.
> – BRUCE LEE

Don't waste your time being miserable and unhappy. Don't let outside circumstances have control over you before you have permission to feel good. The only thing on this planet that will make you feel good and happy is you. Happiness is not about money, nor the large home, or the latest convertible sitting in your garage, depreciating in value.

It's not waiting by the phone for the pretty girl or cute guy you gave your phone number to. It's not about getting the raise from your boss or going on that overseas holiday. It's about enjoying the journey, and what you become in the process. Ask more questions that help you find meaning and inner purpose. Don't seek the approval of others to achieve your happiness either, because they can't give it to you, only you can! You simply make the choice.

> You're happiest while you're making the greatest contribution.
> – ROBERT F KENNEDY

RECLAIM YOUR LIFE

As long as you live like this, you're being dependent on circumstances that are out of your control. You'll always live hot or cold, down or up, happy or sad. This is no way to live, waiting for happiness to arrive. Relax and let go, reclaim your life, take control, it's your choice on how happy you want to be. Not somebody else's.

LITTLE CAT

Here's a fable about happiness, and chasing after it.

> A big cat saw a little cat chasing its tail one day and asked, "Why are you chasing your tail?" The kitten said, "I have learned that the best thing for a cat is happiness, and that happiness is my tail. Therefore, I am chasing it: and when I catch it, I shall have happiness." The big cat said, "My son, I too have paid attention to the problems of the universe. I, too, have judged that happiness is in my tail. But, I have noticed that whenever I chase after it, it keeps running away from me, and when I go about my business throughout the day, it just seems to follow me wherever I go."

Live your life simply. Let the small moments in your life fill you with inner nourishment and joy. Don't let your ego take over, simplify your life and happiness will follow you wherever you go.

> Few things are needed to make a wise man happy; nothing can make a fool content; that is why most men are miserable.
> – LA ROCHEFOUCAULD

DETACH YOURSELF

Detach yourself from everything, including outcomes, money and material possessions. Stop seeking self-approval from people, because if you're attached you're only putting up road blocks to stop the flow of energy coming into your life. This is where opportunity, growth and independence comes into your life, which are the real ingredients for inner fulfilment. It's not the chase of more money, material possessions and prestige, here you're moving away from inner fulfilment, not towards it.

> Pleasure can be supported by illusion, while happiness rests upon truth.
> – NICOLAS CHAMFORT

When people become desperate, they become attached emotionally and they lose their perspective, vision and focus and can't see the good which surrounds them. Appreciate everything and attach yourself to nothing. Change your thoughts and beliefs about situations, change your perceptions and look for the good in everything. It's funny, one person might notice a weed, but to someone else they see a beautiful flower. Understand you become what you think about most of the time, so be happy, love yourself and stay positive.

NOURISH YOUR INNER SELF

Nourish your inner self with all the natural pleasures that life has to offer. These can include all the beauty that surrounds you, the beach, and the rainforest, all of life's natural architecture. Or, view the wonderful paintings in your national art gallery of Matisse, Van Gogh and Goya, and stare in wonder of such creativity these artists were gifted with. Read pieces of literature or classic poems by Wordsworth, Shakespeare or Yeats. Fall in love with your family and people who love you, and cherish your special moments together. Take the time to share a meal together and talk about your day. By bringing back the simple things and appreciating life's wonders and the beauty and love that surrounds you, you can fill your inner well, and be in a state of profound emotional balance.

> Though we travel the world over to find the beautiful, we must carry it with us, or we find it not.
> – RALPH WALDO EMERSON

Choose what you want to see in your life and choose your thoughts, life is already beautiful. It is you that must change, it all starts from the inside. Happiness doesn't arrive like a parcel in the post, or like an unexpected visitor to your home. However, you breathe happiness, and it's a part of you, it's a choice. Stop looking! Because, it's not out there!

> When we do not find peace of mind in ourselves,
> it is useless to seek it elsewhere.
> — *LA ROCHEFOUCAULD*

SEVENTEEN
It's time to self-actualise

> A musician must make music, an artist must paint, a poet must write, if he is to be ultimately at peace with himself. What a man can be he must be. This need we may call self-actualisation.
> – ABRAHAM MASLOW

As this book draws to a close, you will be feeling really good about who you are and I know that you've come a long way from who you used to be. Congratulations. I'm really proud of you. By becoming all that you can be it gives you a sense of achievement and a knowing, you're destined for so many great highs in your life. By putting yourself out there and facing your fears, you get a real sense of self and who you truly are. By testing your limits, mentally and physically you come to understand anything is possible, if you set your mind to it. This is what it means to be a self-actualiser.

> A man's character is his guardian divinity.
> – HERACLITUS

It was Abraham Maslow, an academic psychologist who made the term self-actualisation a common concept. Maslow's hierarchy of needs is represented by a pyramid with the basic needs at the bottom and the need for humans to be what they must be, at the pinnacle or top of the pyramid.

To get to the top of the pyramid and become a self-actualiser, you must first achieve the stages of growth and have all the other needs taken care of first. These are your physiological needs, the basic needs at the bottom of the pyramid and moving up the pyramid to safety, love, belonging and esteem. By having these needs met, your very being will resonate with the same frequency to what you want to achieve in your life, and all of your desires and motivations will adjust just like a domino effect to make your whole complete.

> When the fight begins within himself, a man's worth something.
> – ROBERT BROWNING

By stepping out of your comfort zone, breaking the chains of conformity, and waking up to a new dawn, you now come to realise that you're a creator. The life you have now has come into affect by your thoughts and actions, how you see yourself and by putting the knowledge and your developed skills into the life that you have created. Enjoy who you are, love what you do, be a vessel for love in action to work through you.

See yourself standing on top of the mountain that you have climbed by your sheer determination and persistence, realise your worth, it's your birthright to be happy to devote your life to a higher calling. Nobody apart from yourself has made you come this far.

> No man is free who hasn't mastered himself.
> – EPICTETUS

SAY YES TO CHANGE

Take this belief, this picture which you hold of yourself so strongly and embrace life, say yes to change. Let every moment of your life be special, because you are. Believe that all your needs will be met on every level, be honest with yourself for what you think and feel. Don't let anyone discourage you from finding your higher calling and knowing who you really are. March to the beat of your own drum. Be a light unto yourself and be a shining example for all people to see that they can be the best version of themselves, because they're worth it. Just as you are.

HAVE COURAGE

Have the confidence and the courage to stand firm, you'll be no longer easily manipulated by people or circumstances. May you meet every challenge you encounter with a higher awareness and maturity to fully understand you're truly capable to move through adversity and come out the other side a more effective, self-realised human being.

> You will be of as much worth to others as you are to yourself.
> – CICERO

Let your soul burn brightly, may your presence motivate and inspire all people who come into contact with you. By breaking out of the mould which society has tried to suffocate you in, you have become like a child replacing your fears with pure innovation and creativity. You now know you don't need the approval of others to be happy. By letting go of all your baggage and becoming more real and listening and following your heart's desires, illusion will be lost and your truth will be discovered.

> The only way of discovering the limits of the possible
> is to venture a little way past them into the impossible.
> – ARTHUR C. CLARKE

Make yourself proud by fulfilling all your needs, it's your God given right. You must push your limits, appreciate everything. Discover that your life is to be lived, not lived through. You don't have to justify your actions to anyone. You don't need permission to live out your dreams. You're not a child; you no longer need to look for the self-approval of others. Go forth and be what you must become. Your life and what you do with it, it's yours to direct. Don't let anyone control your destiny. Take control and be all that you can be…now!

> Man, if thou art aught, strive to walk alone and hold converse with yourself, instead of skulking in the chorus! At length think; look around thee; bestir thyself, that thou mayest know who thou art!
> – EPICTETUS

EIGHTEEN
A spiritual tonic

Just as a candle cannot burn without fire,
men cannot live without a spiritual life.
– BUDDHA

Have a question in mind with your eyes closed. When you open your eyes, focus on the list below. When you open your eyes, the first phrase that you notice will be the answer to your questions. Or, just read through the inspiring messages to uplift your spirits!

When you arise in the morning, throughout the day and before you go to bed, let these powerful phrases sink into your subconscious mind. Take in their powerful vibrations and let them resonate with your very being, let them uplift your spirits and encourage you to transform your life.

We're connected to everything

Let go of your ego

Live a new reality

Change your routine

Explore new dimensions of yourself

Free yourself of programming and conditioning

Become self-reliant

Ask yourself, what do I want?

Be independent of other people's opinions

March to the beat of your own drum

Listen to your heart

Don't control others

Be authentic

Be daring and courageous

Do your best

A spiritual tonic

Transform yourself
Believe how powerful you are
Open your arms and embrace change
Be gentle with yourself
Take chances like a child
Live life on purpose
Be all you can be
Be at peace with yourself and everyone
Trust yourself
Don't resist, respond
Live your dreams awake
Approve of yourself now
Storms always end and the rainbow is always ready to shine
Become the person you want to be
Let go of your self-importance
Let go of your fears and trust the process
Don't be trivial
Don't judge or label
Manifest what you want
Follow your heart
Become a silent sage
Tap into the source
Act abundantly in your life
Nurture yourself and others
Believe in yourself
Choose life
Be here now
Forgive
Have faith and trust
Empower yourself and others

Admire beauty
Be happy now
Embrace silence
Let go of resentment and anger
Let go of your destructive thoughts
Be in charge of your own life today
No more excuses
Let go of the past
Know that you are capable
Your possibilities are endless
Dare to face the unknown
Be kind to yourself
Be your message
We're all teachers
People who push our buttons are our real teachers
Never give up
You're beautiful
Be better than you used to be
Treasure yourself and your life
Be love in action
There are no tomorrows, or yesterdays, only todays
Trust the process
Be flexible, not rigid
You can control your efforts, not your outcomes
Be daring today
Explore, dream, discover
Become accountable
Take responsibility for your life
Take action now
You can do it

NINETEEN
Death bed visions

> When I stand before God at the end of my life, I would hope that I would not have a single bit of talent left, and could say 'I used everything you gave me.'
> – ERMA BOMBECK

Let's fast forward your life for a moment. I want you to shut your eyes and visualise yourself on your deathbed with an hour of your physical life to go, before you graduate back to the spirit world and leave your family and friends and all your worldly possessions behind.

This exercise is to put your life into perspective and for you to get your priorities in order for what really matters to you. What's important to you? What would be going through your mind at this time? Do you think it would be all your material possessions that you worked so hard for? Would it be how you worked such long hours in the office, running your immune system down and getting stressed to complete a project to appease the boss? Or would your thoughts turn to having not spent enough quality time with your family and your children or your close friends? Which would have been closer and more meaningful to your heart?

> The tragedy of a man's life is what dies inside of him while he lives.
> – HENRY DAVID THOREAU

Do you think it will be the trivial things, like office gossip, the judging and the criticising that maybe you participated in? Would that matter to you now? Or the way you handled certain situations just to make yourself look good in front of other people to gain popularity points or to win self-approval from others? Or will it be the amount of years you wasted not talking to your loved ones or people you had personality clashes with because your ego was too big to come down to reality? Put yourself in someone else's shoes, show compassion and forgiveness and go with the flow. Have you ever asked yourself the question could I have handled that situation better?

> Wisdom consists in performing only useful actions.
> – CHERBULIEZ

LIFE REVIEW

When you review your life, I wish that you can look at all the great times, the memories and moments that you experienced and shared with the people that mattered most to you. Not only with loved ones but strangers as well, your fellow brothers and sisters and the connections you made in this classroom called life. Did you live your life with integrity and good morals? Did you love unconditionally and turn the other cheek, or were you resentful and bitter? I hope you lived with compassion, love, courtesy and treated people with respect, just like you wanted to be treated without segregation, labels or being judged and criticised for being different to someone like yourself.

When your party is over and your curtain is just about to close, I hope you had enough courage and ambition to live out your ideas and see them come to fruition. How about your dreams, did you make them your reality? Did you express how you felt towards the people you loved? Did you show your emotions or did you bite your tongue and suppress your true self? Now that would be a shame, wouldn't it?

> Life would be infinitely happier if we could be born at
> the age of eighty and gradually approach eighteen.
> – MARK TWAIN

What about your fears? Did you feel the fear and continue? Or, did you stay in your comfort zone and let someone else control your destiny? When you are having trouble making a decision or taking a risk, or want to step out into the unknown and having trouble doing so, ask yourself this question. How long am I going to be dead for? I hope that clears things up for you!

> Somebody should tell us, right at the start of our lives,
> that we are dying. Then we might live life to the limit, every
> minute of every day. Do it! I say, whatever you want to do,
> do it now! There are only so many tomorrows.
> – MICHAEL LANDON

As I'm writing this and putting pen to paper, I'm thinking about my own mortality and how I'm living life. I can honestly say if I was to die tomorrow, (I hope not, I've still got so much to do!) I have lived out my dreams, I'm a self-made man, and I've encouraged thousands of people to believe in themselves. I've been of service to the community that I live in. I've given, received and learnt from my mistakes. My soul has evolved and I have enjoyed playing my role being Luke Edward Sheedy and I didn't die with the music still in me! I wish the same for you.

I walk past the cemetery and I can't help but wonder did all these people live out their dreams and aspirations? Did they turn their inventions and ideas into a reality? I hoped they believed in themselves and others as much as I do, and I hope for you. I wished that they developed their strengths, abilities and talents and used up everything they had, before they found out it was too late.

> I did not wish to live what was not life, living is so dear.
> – HENRY DAVID THOREAU

While I was finishing writing this book, my beautiful wife gave me a fantastic book to conclude my chapter on Death Bed Visions. It's written by Bronnie Ware, called *The Top Five Regrets of the Dying: A Life Transformed by the Dearly Departing*. Bronnie worked in palliative care and her job entailed taking care of the dying. In this book she explains the top five regrets her patients had while in her care and what they would do if they had their chance again. The five regrets that her patients told her were:

1. "I wish I'd had the courage to live a life true to myself, not the life others expected of me."
2. "I wish I hadn't worked so hard."
3. "I wish I'd had the courage to express my feelings."
4. "I wish I had stayed in touch with my friends."
5. "I wish I had let myself be happier."

By reading and understanding Bronnie's patients' regrets you can make a positive change in your life by adding any of these issues you have in your own life. When you do this you'll be inspired to take control of your life today, before it's too late. The book is a must-read for anybody who wants to live their life more effectively.

Discover Your Path

> Where there is no vision, the people perish...
> – PROVERB 29:18

Open up to a larger vision for yourself in your life. Imagine all the great things you want in your life, and see them coming to you. Don't stay in your comfort zone, get out from underneath your security blanket. You have to believe there is a big, beautiful world out there just waiting for you to enjoy and explore it. Just like this fable below suggests.

LITTLE FROG IN THE WELL

There was a little frog that lived at the bottom of a deep, dark well filled with shallow water and moss-covered walls. When the frog was hungry or thirsty, he ate insects or drank from the well. When he was tired, he slept on small rocks. In between, he would watch the sky above and see the passing clouds. Even though he had never left his well, he was satisfied.

When the birds would fly overhead, the frog would beckon them to join him, "It's so pleasant down here, I have cool water to drink and insects to eat, and at night I watch the stars and the moon." The birds would reply that the world is much bigger and more beautiful than his well. However, little frog insisted that nothing could be better than his well.

The birds eventually stopped visiting little frog due to his stubbornness, even though he didn't understand why. Little frog was lonely until a bluebird stopped at the edge of the well. Little frog encouraged her to visit his home. She flew away without responding, and continued this every day for a week. Finally, bluebird asked to show the frog the outside world. However, he refused and the bluebird became so infuriated, she flew to the bottom, picked up the little frog and flew out of the well.

For the first time, the little frog saw bright sunshine, mountains and valleys, rivers and the sea. He realised there was an abundance of food and water as well as nature in all its splendour including beautiful flowers, trees, fruits and other creatures and animals in the world.

Overwhelmed by the beauty, little frog finally cried out in happiness, "Thankyou bluebird for opening my eyes to this magnificent world that exists beyond my well." Little frog vowed never to go back to his deep, dark well ever again.

No-one gets out of here alive, it doesn't matter what you have or haven't got. What matters is what you think of yourself, did you do your best? Look at your life are you watching in the audience taking it casually and not getting involved or are you out on the stage of life participating, being all that you can be? Did you explore yourself? Did you go out into the wilderness called life and learn about yourself?

Just like the little frog in the well, did you open up your vision, and discover all life in all its beauty and glory? Do you really know thy self? When you walked down the highway called life and came to an intersection did you choose security or did you take the road less travelled? In your last moments of this physical incarnation you can quietly say to yourself, "I dreamed big and opened up my vision."

> Every day to wise man is a new life.
> — SENECA

Okay, now draw your attention and focus to the present moment. Guess what, you're still alive, isn't it wonderful? You've been reborn, a second chance. Enjoy this moment, just like your next breath, its precious isn't it?

Well then, the only time is now, dream, explore, discover — because you're worth it and you're alive. Don't waste it, embrace it. Because it's your turn, so what are you going to do about it?

> It's time to start living the life you've imagined.
> — HENRY JAMES

TWENTY
Your next chapter

> While there's life, there's hope.
> — MARCUS TULLIUS CICERO

I believe this is the most important chapter of all, because now it's your turn. You can only read so much information to gain knowledge. If you don't do and act on what you've read about, why bother, it's just another self-development book to be placed on the book case to collect dust. Make this book the pivot of your collection, the one that changed your life. All of my feelings, knowledge, experiences, thoughts and actions have led me to write this book for you. I took the next step in my life, will you do the same?

> He who has begun has half done. Dare to be wise; begin!
> — HORACE

I have never written a book before, let alone kept a journal. But I had the inner desire and motivation to sit down every day, many nights and weekends to share with you what I know and have learnt. My experiences, my life, and what has worked for me, I know will help you as well. I love people and I love life, if you want to start a new chapter, a new beginning, start now, as Les Brown says, "If you want to take it casually, you'll end up a casualty!"

> At the day of judgement, we shall not be asked
> what we have read, but what we have done.
> — THOMAS A KEMPIS

When I was a young boy growing up, no-one in my family ever encouraged me or told me that they believed in me. I went out and worked hard to build my self-confidence and self-esteem, and in doing this developed a very strong self-worth, I'm a self-made man. I didn't ride daddy's coat tails and I wasn't born with a silver spoon in my mouth but I had a true desire and will to live the life of my dreams.

> Who then is free? The wise man who has dominion over himself.
> – HORACE

I know what it's like to be lost, to be afraid and scared and not having a clue about what to do with the life you have. But in this book I have laid down the foundation, laid a path for you to take hold of your life, to get up and get going. It will help you find your direction, your path, your purpose and meaning to get up each morning and embrace this wonderful gift.

I truly believe if you take notes and read this book with enthusiasm and gusto, just in the spirit in which it was written for you, it will open your mind and give you the encouragement you need to live your life with enthusiasm and excitement. It will make you understand you are more than worthy, that you have the right just like anybody else out there to be happy, and fulfilled from the inside out.

> Learning dissipates many doubts, and causes many things otherwise invisible to be seen and is the eye of everyone who is not absolutely blind.
> – HITOPADESHA

I have written this book for humankind for future generations, this is my legacy to you. We're all in this together we come to this school called life. For the most of us, not knowing where from, or what the hell are we going to do or how long we're here for. But why not be the best you can be? You've been given such a wonderful gift of life. You owe it to yourself to live it as you see it. I only want the best for you, love, happiness and deep inner fulfilment.

I BELIEVE IN YOU

But you know what? I truly believe in you, that you are capable of being the best that you can be. If you have the willpower, perseverance and the commitment to develop your strengths and abilities you'll fall in love with yourself. When you begin this a change will occur, your worth and esteem will increase and you'll start climbing to inner and outer heights that you thought weren't imaginable. You must give it a go, otherwise you'll never know! This is your life, nothing is more precious than that.

Falling in love with yourself is a beautiful thing, you're beautiful, you must know this. And when you do, you'll receive love and give love unconditionally.

This is another reason why you're a short term resident here on Earth, to know and experience it. We're all part of a much bigger picture. Drop your ego and be free of all attachments because your true calling awaits you. This is the true meaning of your life, become active, you must play your part, don't be afraid or passive, be heroic and brave.

> Heaven is under our feet as well as over our heads.
> – HENRY DAVID THOREAU

Life is all about learning, discovering new passions, hobbies and interests and putting yourself out there to discover other dimensions of yourself.

I learnt while writing this book, that I truly love writing, it's so liberating. I know now I have the dedication, persistence and stamina to sit down every day to write. I've also learnt that if you want change in your life and you're sick of having much more of the same, you'll let go of fear, embrace change and be reborn into a new exciting life for yourself. This is your life, make the decision. What have you got to lose, take a look around right now, do you want more of this? It's time to take the plunge, I have and now it's your turn.

> He who asks of life nothing but the improvement of how his own nature and a continuous good progress towards inner contentment and spiritual submission, is less likely than anyone else to miss and waste life.
> – HENRI FREDERIC AMIEL

TWENTY-ONE
My best wishes

To be, or not to be, that is the question.
— SHAKESPEARE

Writing this book has been the most rewarding thing I have ever achieved, apart from marrying my beautiful wife and best friend, Julia.

This book was written from my heart to you. Although I might not know you, what I do know is that you're special, just like me. We're all walking this path together, some of you may have just started your journey, maybe I'm just in front of you, and others I can see in the far distance.

It doesn't really matter, in the end we all arrive at our destinations. Some have an easy route and others take the road less travelled, some like to take the long road, but that's ok too! Sometimes life does get unstable and treacherous and other times it's easy and fun, but to really grow and evolve you must keep going, especially when it gets tough. This is where real growth and change manifests, understand you're worth it.

Judy, a psychic I met long ago, you may have forgotten me, but I remember you. You told me 18 years ago, that I would write a book to encourage people to believe in themselves. Well this is it, your prophecy came true.

To all the people who have read this book, I hope it has encouraged you to take that important step, to embrace life and be all that you can be. My gift to you has been the seeds of higher consciousness that I have passed onto you throughout this book. So now, your life will produce beautiful fruits of labour and attract a wonderful harvest of abundance in all aspects of your life. Remember, you reap what you sow.

I have a bit of a tear in my eye now, it's been a while since that happened. These are true tears of joy. This is a new beginning, for me as well. I hope I get to meet you someday real soon. Make sure you say hello to me and tell me what my book has done to encourage you to change your life. I look forward to hearing all about your happiness and success. I'm sure our paths will cross sometime soon.

To purchase this as an e-book, audio book, or to attend a workshop or private consultation, visit **www.lukesheedy.com**.

I'd love to hear how this book has changed your life, visit my website or if you'd like to write, please address mail to:

>Inner Knowing Publishing
>PO Box 1291
>Stafford QLD
>AUSTRALIA, 4053.

If you want change in your life and to live the life that is congruent with what's most important to you, as Max Lucado says, "To lead the orchestra, you have to turn your back on the crowd." Be original, be independent, but most importantly, believe in yourself!

Let me be the first one to tell you, to all those people who have not been told this before…YOU'RE IMPORTANT, YOU MATTER, I BELIEVE IN YOU AND I ENCOURAGE YOU TO GO FOR IT, BECAUSE YOU'RE WORTH IT.

Peace and harmony
Luke Edward Sheedy
Summer 2012

> The law of harvest is to reap more than you sow.
> Sow an act, and you reap a habit.
> Sow a habit, and you reap a character.
> Sow a character, and you reap a destiny.
> – MARK TWAIN

It's time to believe in yourself

It's time for you to believe in yourself, my friend
To truly learn to know thyself, til the end
It's time to let go of the programming that makes you forget who you are
It's you and me, who is the star
It's time for you to discover all your hidden treasures
Which God has given you, to find life's hidden pleasures
Your talents, abilities and strength are yours to be had
And nobody else's, so please be glad
This is your life, so don't ever be discouraged
In life, it's always nice, to be encouraged
Love and respect all those that you meet
For we are all brothers and sisters, so I can't wait 'til we meet
You are beautiful and perfect in your own unique way
I just want to say, why not do it, your own sweet way
May your self worth and esteem be strong
I want you to know, you belong
Did you know you're a creator?
It's time for you to start right now, not later
Your magical life is at hand
It's time for you, to take a stand
Open your mind and you will surely see, it is you, who is now truly free
Every moment is special, don't you see?
It's time to dream, and create your new reality
Live in the moment and enjoy your life
So don't ponder on despair, trouble or strife

Discover Your Path

When you make the decision to act
You now know it is you, who controls your life
It's time for me to go now, my new friend
I've strengthened your inner vision, right up til the end
May your life be full of love and adventure
Because in the end, I don't want you to ponder
I hope you've loved my book, I can clearly see
It was a sacred contract between you and me
Just one more thing before we depart
I believe in you, and this is only the start

With love,
Luke Edward Sheedy

Glossary of terms

Affirmation — the practice of positive attitude or statement that should be repeated to oneself, written down in the present. It must be positive, personal and specific

Alchemist — a person who has manifested or changed mentally, emotionally, physically or spiritually to a better version of themselves

Aura — a field of subtle, luminous radiation surrounding a person or object

Chakra — energy centres of the body from which a person can collect energy, they correspond to vital points in the physical body and are connected to major organs or glands that govern other body parts

Consciousness — the quality or state of being aware of an external object or something within oneself, the ability to experience or to feel

Cosmic Consciousness — the ideal that the universe exists as an interconnected network of consciousness, with each conscious being linked to every other

Dimension — many different realities occupying the same space but on a different frequency

Enlightenment — refers to the full comprehension of a situation, the emancipation of the human consciousness from an immature state of ignorance and error

Intuition — the ability to acquire knowledge from within oneself

Mantra — a sound, syllable, word or group of words that is considered capable of creating transformation

Natural law — determined by nature and is universal; the use of reason to analyse personal and social human nature

Subconscious mind — the part of the mind below the level of conscious perception. Subconscious thoughts are activities of the mind which we are not always consciously aware of

Universal energy – the life force that permeates all living and non-living things

Universal law — principles and rules for governing human beings' conduct

Universal mind — the higher consciousness or source of being, it's the belief that one has access to all knowledge known and unknown

Suggested reading

Over the years I have read many books; too many to mention and I have come across some books that I really enjoyed and which struck a chord with me. They helped open my eyes and mind to a higher consciousness and understanding. If you enjoy human potential and spiritual books focusing on higher awareness and the betterment of oneself, I recommend the books below.

Celestine Prophecy, James Redfield
Feel the Fear And Do It Anyway, Susan Jeffers
Hands of Healing, Barbara Brennan
Man's Search for Meaning, Vicktor E Frankl
Power VS Force, David R. Hawkins
Psycho-Cybernetics, Maxwell Maltz
The Alchemist, Paul Coelho
The Art of Happiness, Dalai Lama and Howard C. Cutler
The Power of Positive Thinking, Norman Vincent Peale
*The Top Five Regrets of the Dying:
A Life Transformed by the Dearly Departing*, Bronnie Ware
Thick Face Black Heart, Chin-Ning Chu
Think and Grow Rich, Napoleon Hill
Walden, Henry David Thoreau
Way of the Peaceful Warrior, Dan Millman

Bibliography

Adamo, Peter 2004, *Eat Right for Your Type*. New York/USA: Penguin Putnam Inc.

Australian Bureau of Statistics. *National Survey of Health and Wellbeing*, 2007. Catalogue number 4326, Australian Bureau of Statistics, Canberra.
_____, *Year Book Australia 2009-10*. Catalogue number 1301, Australian Bureau of Statistics, Canberra.

Clarke, Arthur C., 1962, Hazards of Prophecy: The Failure of Imagination, in *Profiles of the Future*. New York/USA: Harper and Row.

Cummings, E. E 1938, *Collected Poems*. USA: Harcourt, Brace, & World, Inc.

De Saint-Exupery, Antoine 1946, *Le Petit Prince*. Translated by Katherine Woods. France: Houghton Mifflin Harcourt.

Einstein, Albert. Quotes reprinted with permission from the Hebrew University of Jerusalem.

Emoto, Masaru 2004, *The Hidden Messages in Water*. Oregon/USA: Beyond Words Publishing. Original Japanese edition published by Sunmark Publishing, 2001.

Ford, Henry 1926, *Ford News* March 1, 1926, pp. 2.

Gide, Andre 1973, *The Counterfeiters*. Paris/France: Vintage.

Gibran, Khalil 2010, *The Prophet*. USA: Martino Fine Books.

Hawkins, David R., 1995, *Power VS Force*. Arizona/USA: Veritas Publishing, pp. 29-30, 71, 96-102. www.veritaspub.com.

Hay, Louise L. 2006, *Life!: Reflections on Your Journey*. Carlsbad/USA: Hay House, Inc.

Hill, Napoleon 2010, *Think and Grow Rich*. Hollywood/USA: Simon and Brown.

http://www.betterhealth.vic.gov.au

http://www.ntpages.com.au

http://www.who.int/mental_health/prevention/suicide

Jung, Carl 1977, *Mysterium Coniunctionis* (Collected Works of C.G Jung Vol 14). Princeton/USA: Princeton University Press.

Johnston, C. 1972, *To See the World in a Grain of Sand*. Norwalk, Conn/USA: C R Gibson Co, pp. 13 "On happiness" (The Little Cat Fable) by C.L James.

Maslow, Abraham and Frager, Robert 1954, *Motivation and Personality*. New York/USA: Harper and Row.

Nightingale, Earl 2012, *The Strangest Secret*. USA:lulu.com.

Rohn, Jim 2006, *The Treasury of Quotes by Jim Rohn*, America's Foremost Business Philosopher. Reprinted with permission from Jim Rohn International © 2011.

Sawyer, M.G. et al., Child and adolescent component of the National Survey of Mental Health and Wellbeing. ACT/Australia: Mental Health and Special Programs Branch of the Commonwealth Department of Health and Aged Care.

Schwartz, Morrie 1996, *Morrie: In His Own Words: Life Wisdom From a Remarkable Man*. USA: Bloomsbury Publishing Plc.

Shedd, John, A., 1928, *Salt from My Attic*. Portland, Main/USA: Mosher Press.

The Holy Bible, King James Version. New York: Oxford Edition: 1769; *King James Bible Online*, 2008.

Ware, Bronnie 2012, *The Top Five Regrets of the Dying: A Life Transformed by the Dearly Departing*. Carlsbad/USA: Hay House Inc.

Wilson, Harold January 23 1967, *Speech to the Consultative Assembly of the Council of Europe, Strasbourg, France* and reported in The New York Times, January 24, 1967.

Wooden, John and Jamison, Steve 1997, *A Lifetime of Observations and Reflections On and Off the Court*. USA: McGraw-Hill.

Wittgenstein, Ludwig 2009, *Philosophical Investigations*. Revised Fourth Edition by P.M.S Hacker and Joachim Schulte. United Kingdom: John Wiley & Sons.

www.ingramcontent.com/pod-product-compliance
Lightning Source LLC
Chambersburg PA
CBHW051434290426
44109CB00016B/1547